THE IMITATION OF SANKARA

BEING

(A COLLECTION OF SEVERAL
TEXTS BEARING ON THE ADVAITA)

THE IMITATION OF SANKARA

BEING

(A COLLECTION OF SEVERAL

TEXTS BEARING ON THE ADVAITA)

BY

MANILAL. N. DVIVEDI.

GYAN

Published by

Gyan Publishing House
5, Ansari Road
Daryaganj, New Delhi-110002
Phone: 011-47034999, 9811692060
E-mail: books@gyanbooks.com

Distribution Network
gyanbooks.com
India, USA, Canada, UK, Australia, France

ISBN : 978-81-212-2250-1 (PB)
First Published, 1895

2nd Impression 2021

Printed at: Gyan Press, Delhi.

The Imitation of Sankara
Author: Manilal. N. Dvivedi

THE IMITATION OF S'ANKARA.

BEING

(A COLLECTION OF SEVERAL TEXTS BEARING ON THE ADVAITA)

BY

MANILAL. N. DVIVEDI.

1895.

INDIA: BOMBAY: PANDIT JYESTARAM MUKUNDJI, KALBADEVI ROAD.

N. M. & CO., KALBADEVI ROAD.

NADIAD: SUDARS'ANA OFFICE.

LONDON: GEORGE REDWAY, 9, HART STREET, BLOOMSBURY.

वसिष्ठः—

युक्तियुक्तमुपादेयं वचनं बालकादपि ।
अन्यत्तृणमिव त्याज्यमप्युक्तं पद्मजन्मना ॥ यो० वा० ॥

VASISHTHA :—

" Hear even a child and accept the truth that goes " straight to thy heart ; leave all else aside, even like " so much straw, though the lotus-born Creator were " the speaker."—*Yogavâsishtha.*

CONTENTS.

INTRODUCTION.

"In the whole world there is no study so beneficial and "so elevating as that of the *Upanishads.* It has been the "solace of my life, it will be the solace of my death." These words of the German sage were cheerfully endorsed, only last year, by a living scholar and thinker of considerable repute and authority. The Philosophy of the *Upanishads* scarcely needs recommendation. Philosophers from Plato to Schopenhauer are unanimous in their testimony to the elevating, alleviating, influence of the *Vedânta.* An Age of Positive Science alone requires to be put in mind of these expressions.

It has been the ambition of my heart, from the first-hand experience I have had of the truth of these remarks, to present the main Idea of this sublime universal 'Philosophy of the Absolute' in as simple and popular a form as the nature of the subject would permit. The deservedly popular book of Thomas-a-Kempis, 'The Imitation of Christ,' fascinated my attention, and Bowdon's 'Imitation of Buddha' suggested the plan of this work. There was the same mighty spirit breathing in the child of Galilee, the prince of Kapilavastu, and this *Brâhmaṇa* of Southern India. He has as much right to an 'Imitation' as the other seers of antiquity; the need for an 'Imitation of S'ankara' is perhaps greatest in the present day.

I am not unconscious of the defects of my performance. It lacs the simplicity of Kempis. The nature of the subject is my only excuse; and if the book gives plain, serious, earnest, matter for thought, at first sight, I should consider it no small satisfaction. Then again the detached nature of the information is another difficulty in the way. Loss of context might occasionally tend to obscure the sense of a passage. I have, however, tried to remedy this defect by stringing the pieces together in a kind of fictitious context from end to end. Many of the passages could have been given in much better language, for, several of them have been translated before by abler hands ; but I have my reasons for attempting fresh translation.* Where commentaries have been available, I have carefully consulted them, and, by giving a free rendering of every text, I have done my best to combine the spirit of the context and the strength of the commentary in my translation. Among commentaries those of S'ankara have always had the preference. In one more respect does this work differ from that of Kempis or rather that of Bowdon. The collection here is not entirely from the works of S'ankara, but from all works bearing on the Philosophy taught by S'ankara and his followers. I have divided the whole collection into sections and sub-sections with a view to exhaust the main topics of the Absolute Philosophy. Texts from the *Upanishads* and other works are often referred to in *Vedânta*-writings. That almost every important reference of this kind may easily be traced to its place in this collection, where it should be found in its entirety with translation, a careful Alphabetical Index has been appended at the end. Another Index puts together the principal points of this Philosophy, and directs even the most casual reader to whatever information this book can give on the question and its bearings. Words not Englished in the text have been collected together for explanation in an Index, to which the reader may conveniently refer.

With the chapter of genesis thus finished, we may take closer view of the child that sees the light. Many a reader would, however, be curious to hear something of the god-father of this infant. A few words can satisfy the curiosity, for, it is matter of secondary consequence in a work of this kind to concern ourselves with the yet disputed question of the history of S'ankara. We are here concerned with the mighty spirit underlying the shell bearing that name, with the

* For instance, just turn to para 94. Prof. Max Müller renders it thus at page 137 of his 'Three Lectures on the Vedânta :' "This is the light of lights, when it shines the sun does not shine, nor the moon and the stars, nor lightenings, much less this fire. When *Brahman* shines everything shines after him, by his light all the world is lighted."

awakening, enchanting music of the harmony through which It relates itself to posterity and time. It is not certain when S'ankara lived ; some place him after, some before Christ. He was a *Brâhmaṇa*, native of some obscure town on the coast of Malabar. He is reported to be an incarnation of god S'iva. He found the Light while yet eight years of age, and, with the permission of his fond mother, he renounced the world and became a *Sannyâsin.* Through Renunciation he transferred the sphere of his activity from the narrow limits of his simple homestead to the wide expanse of interesting humanity and the world. He solved the national problem of the day through his Philosophy which exercised a powerful, potent charm over the mind of India. The victorious termination of his universal philosophic war made him the one *Âchârya*, the one master-philosopher of the land. He founded four mighty 'seats of learning (*Mathas*)' in the four corners of India. These are extant to the present day. The body which encaged this mighty spirit was dissolved at the early age of thirty-two.

He has composed several works in poetry and prose, the latter all commentaries. Fascinating, weird music ; lucid, chaste, powerful, balanced expression; universal, unsectarian, fearless, loving exposition;—these are some of the characteristics of his varied literary style. He was a real master of the Philosophy he preached ; he can express it in half a verse, or a quarto volume of many hundred pages. He would readily break a lance with any adversary, atheist, materialist, ritualist, magician, ascetic, *Yogi*, or *Tântric.* His writings largely reflect the spirit of the age he lived in ; but the magic of the master whose wand can weld all difference into the homogeneous unity of his spell is unmistakable throughout. The glory of his literary activity is his gloss on the *Upanishads,* the *Bhagvad-Gitâ* and the *Brahma-sutras*, to say nothing of the numerous poems, large and small, which survive on the lip of many a follower of the *Vedânta* to the present day. The permanent charm of his name lives undoubtedly in the Absolute Philosophy he taught then and for ever to India and the world at large. These, divested of the stirring and the miraculous which inseparably gather round the life of every great spiritual teacher, are the bare facts of the history of the greatest philosopher the world has ever seen.*

One thing is clear from the records we have of this great teacher. India was divided into a number of religious sects, the people were torn into a number of castes, and the dry forms of ritualism were crushing all spirit out of the true Ideal of the *Veda*. This Ideal lay in the *Advaita*, in the *parâ-vidyâ*, the last esoteric initiation spoken of in the *Upanishads*. The keepers of this Mystery were daily growing jealous of all who, without the necessary training, tried to lift the veil in idle curiosity. Those who caught glimpse of the Truth had not the strength to bear its glare. They interpreted it in the language of physical speech, and mistook the Ideal in the disgusting orgies of the Left-hand-path (*vâma-mârga*). The Lord of Compassion emerging from the princely home at Kapilavastu, found the Light (*Bodhi*) in the Ideal which was thus reserved by tradition for the aspirant who had passed through the necessary forms of practical *Vedic* life and ritual. He proclaimed this openly to the world, without distinction of caste or colour, creed or religion. He preached the law of supreme moral purity and love. In the simple yet sublime universality of his teaching there, however, was no distinct provision for those forms of life and religion which satisfy the wants of ordinary physical intelligence. "Put no faith in momentary things, look upon everything as not-self, find *Nirvâṇa* in the equality of love and peace";—this was the essence of the Lord's teaching. Herein, obviously, was no place for the ordinary masses, for the traditions of the nation. This Ideal was, of course, the true Ideal of the *Veda*, concealed in the *Upanishads*. This is the Ideal perhaps, of all philosophy whatever; but every Ideal carries

* I have in mind Mason's compliment calling Hegel 'the last of the world's great metaphysicians.' In my estimate of S'ankara and his work, I have not lost sight of the great names of philosophy and metaphysics.

with it its own success or doom in the nature of those who receive it.

Chaotic India with this high Ideal before the people called thus to look down upon what formed a most necessary training in the mode of life and religion they had lived through the *Veda* and its tradition, stood the most imminent danger of sinking in hopeless demoralization, stood the most alluring chance of running on the path of utter denationalization and ruin. The distinction between a fool and a philosopher lies more in the wisdom the latter has learnt in the school of experience, than in the external freedom of life he shares in common with any inmate of the madhouse. The Ideal of 'free living' conduces to peace and well-being when found as the fruit of a process of regular spiritual development. Proposed at the very threshold of life, it must lead to atheism, immorality, and consummate hypocrisy. Such, indeed, is human nature. Till the spirit attains the exhaltation whence it can take correct measure of things above and below, high ideals get clogged in the materiality of ordinary give and take ; empty words take place of the Idea which continually escapes ; and mistake in presentation of the Ideal confirms a hundred-fold the very wrong which it was conceived to destroy. This is amply borne out by the fate of Buddhism after the Lord's *Nirvâṇa*.

India was thus on the point of having her past wiped out from history, and with her past the permanent service she renders to the world as a perennial stream of spiritual wisdom and philosophy. This is clearly inferrible from the furious wars this *Bhahmaṇa*-philosopher and reformer waged against the adherents of Bacchanalian *Tântric*-rites on the one hand, and with the obstinate worshippers of dry Formalism on the other. Even the political outlook was neither cheerful nor cheering. With the *Kshatriya* prince of Kapilavastu for guide and teacher the whole of war-like India was in a kind of revolt against itself, against the jealous *Brâhmaṇa* and his spiritual prerogative. An internecine war was most imminent. The spirit of revolt having touched religion and society political order was bound to succumb. Considering the religious, social, political situation, the laurels of time are, in my opinion, fully earned by this *Brâhmaṇa*-reformer for the peaceful revolution he worked through his Philosophy and example.

With the Enlightenment of the nineteenth century about us, we are, almost unconsciously, led into a comparision of those times with these. And the situation is largely suggestive, the points of resemblance strongly inviting, and the mind of the Master worth careful study and Imitation. There is, indeed, sore need of The Imitation of S'ankara all the world over. Let the reader have the picture and its eloquent suggestion before his mind, let him imagine the Master pointing the way to Reform and Peace, and let him seriously construe, in some calm moment, these faltering accents of mine, into the inaudible expression of the Master's mighty melody.

The value of S'ankara's work is not thus historical only. The philosophy he taught and explained is pre-eminently Universal. There is no shade of opinion, no method or discovery of science, no department of experience, which may not find its proper place within the ample folds of the Absolute Philosophy. It is the source of much needed peace and happiness to mankind, it is the law and life of every great action, it is the balm of all evil. One touch of it 'makes the whole world kin.' It puts new life in action, new meaning in words, new vitality in forms, new things in thought. The Absolute Philosophy is the gospel of Nature;— Nature not as understood by dogmatic materialism, but Nature the source and support of all life and all love. It throws a bridge across the wide gulf of country and country, nation and nation, caste and caste, individual and individual. Thus it melts all shadow of separateness into the substance of Unity. Says the Master: "In that Thing, the inner being of all, the billow-less ocean of native bliss and light, what means this nightmare of separateness, creating distinctions of *Brâhmaṇa*, and *Chânḍâla*, and so on." All philosophy has from of old been defined as the search after the one in the many, and if any one has successfully solved the problem of 'one in many,' in its social, religious, political application, it is this one man of his age, S'ankara. Let this universal aspect of his teaching be never absent from the reader's mind.

And in this let spirit address spirit, let not words delude the reader into that false logic which cannot rise beyond the subtleties of physical speech. Consult your consciousness at every step, and try, as a follower of S'ankara well puts it, to "unify the facts of consciousness "with the teachings of philosophy and the teacher's explana-"tions." Words without the corresponding *idea*, not in the outer objective world, but in the inner subjective consciousness, lead to that mad Metaphysics which is the ridicule of Positive Science. On the other hand, words always tied to the physical *fact*, create such artificial limits in the ever unlimited field of knowledge as make Philosophy look down with a sneer upon Science and Agnosticism. Truth lies between these extremes. In the compromise between *fact* and *idea* is the source of all knowledge, all language; too much attachment to one side only of the equation is the fruitful source of false logic and dogmatic reasoning. The law of correspondence is scientifically, also philologically true. Language is but an expression of Thought, of the Spirit that ever tries to reflect and regain itself through forms of language. Every word, every expression has corresponding ideas on all planes of nature—up to the spiritual. You cannot interpret spirit in terms of matter. It is impossible to interpret some fact even of the intellectual plane in language bound to the physical, except by distant analogies and partial comparisons. And how much more must this be true of the plane of distinction-less, character-less universal spirit.*

* This word Spirit is used throughout in the strictly philosophical sense of Essence, the being of things; not the realistic essence apart from things, but the abstract Being wherein all beings partake and exist, *so to speak*.

The only language of describing this Universal, this All without any definite parts or properties, is the language of contradiction. It is and is not, it is everywhere and nowhere, it is everything and nothing, it is being and non-being. The 'Law of Excluded Meddle' cannot grasp It, for It is the law of laws, the logic of logics, the science of sciences. The ultimate fact of the Thing is ever beyond speech, and is best explained, as Yâjnavalkya taught an impertinent pupil repeatedly questioning him on the nature of *Brahman*, by the language of utter Silence. Let the reader be thus put on his guard against the use or rather the misuse of language.

And those who at present or at any time desire a better state of things, social, political, religious, may, thus, well derive a lesson from the way in which S'ankara applied his Philosophy to the problems of his time. Simple as Truth is, it continually escapes because of its simplicity. We realize its glory only when the hand of some master is stretched forth to point to it with authority and vigour. S'ankara showed that in seeking physical unity, in doing away only with the external distinctions of caste and creed, the method of all real practical reform was applied at the wrong end. All reform must proceed from the centre, must work itself out from within. No empire, political, social or moral, can ever stand on mere physical foundation, on brute force, on the outer body alone. The principle of unity which must be sound and substantial to mean strength lies deeper. Sameness of object, identity of purpose might hold men together and carry them beyond the narrow circle of individuality for a time, but that this exhaltation may be permanent, that object and that purpose must be more than skin-deep. Until this is so, efforts at reform and regeneration tend only to compromise and hypocrisy, whatever gilded title they may go under. Physical differences must be sunk in intellectual unity. But even the Intellect is such a treacherous, untrustworthy guide, such a foolish, stupid leader, we are not sure where it will follow in the lead of passions and emotions, and feelings and likes and dislikes. Of Intellect addressing Intellect in the present day there is no end; the results are very meagre, not to say disastrous. Mankind must necessarily soar higher, must find That wherein are drowned the differences of Intellect.

This, says S'ankara, is the Absolute, the Unit, *Brahman*, *Âtman*, Spirit, Idea. Poets and philosophers, the genius and the man of wisdom, sages and prophets, charm by the power they acquire from glimpses of this Unit, in moments when they soar on the wings of Imagination beyond the physical and the Intellectual. The material degeneration of the Roman Empire, the Intellectual imbecility of the forms of heathen religion, led to a chaos which only the magic of the Spirit who had vision of this Unit could instantly call to order. The success which attends this bond of Christianity is before us in the present day. It was reserved for S'ankara to preserve the coherence of the forms of *Vedic* worship. They were already worn thread-bare under the Intellectual hammer, and were fast dissolving under a ray of Light from the one Enlightened Unit of the preceding age. He recognised the Truth of the Lord's teaching, even to the extent of earning for himself the opprobrious title of a Buddha under Brâhmanic garb. But he gave convenient prominence to the difference of intellect and intellect, mind and mind, and made quiet room for distinction in Unity. He added the most necessary supplement to the Ideal of Lord Buddha and effected an easy compromise by showing that all distinctions of sect and belief, class and creed, had each its own place and use in the economy of nature according to the spiritual development it indicated. And yet there was no distinction whatever in the inner thorough unity of all in *Brahman*. Thus he infused fresh life in and gave resisting power to the dying past of the nation, and once more placed on solid foundation, the most ancient and, at the same time, the most universally refined spiritual civilization the world possesses. If history repeats itself, mankind had, in the present day, better learn from history, than waste its trust on intellectual toys and physical non-sense. Through the Unit beyond mind and body lies the way of victory and peace ; in the Unit is the fulfilment of all life and existence ; from the Unit is the law of all activity whatever. Individual differences, personal jealousies, all the imps of passion and emotion, that trifle with great responsibilities, wantonly destroy the glorious gems of Futurity, can never confidently be laid at rest till mankind gains and realizes this Ideal of the Absolute Philosophy.

Let us for a moment try to discern the secret of S'ankara. The Light revealed to weak eyes by the Enlightened Lord Buddha tended more to blur than enlighten vision. The esoteric philosophy in jealous possession of the *Veda* and its keepers was not essentially different from the Light thus proffered ; the difference lay only in the *presentation*. Minds like Gaudapâda and Vyâsa had already found and proclaimed to the world the Absolute Philosophy of the *Upanishads*, of the *Vedânta*—the End of the *Veda*. Epics like the Râmâyaṇa and the Mahâ-Bhârata had already pointed out the path of Unity in diversity, of inaction in action. S'ankara only enlarged upon the materials thus available ; but the way in which he applied this philosophy to the situation reflects immense, undying glory upon the prophetic vision, universal reason, loving heart, and successful tact of the one master-mind which saved the country from running headlong into political chaos, intellectual ruin and spiritual perdition. He at once perceived that the Absolute Philosophy was wide enough to embrace within its bosom every variety of relative thought and life, every shade of distinction and opinion, without disturbing the one-ness of the All. By thus making room for the objective religion which the people always require, he saved Idealism from that obloquy and contempt which hypocrisy and evil born of wrong application would naturally have heaped upon it, and would thus have driven it away from the country or held it up, as in modern Europe, to the permanent ridicule of the world and its wisdom. For once and only once in the history of Philosophy has Idealism thus been successful in practically solving a very intricate national problem ; and herein lies, in my opinion, S'ankara's title to 'the greatest philosopher the world has ever seen.' And in this historical proof of the success of Idealism is the hope of its future. India and the world at large must find salvation and relief from all the ills of the present, in a fresh application of this philosophy to the situation. And this not once but for ever and anon in all time to come. That is the key we have to thank S'ankara for.

The distinction between Philosophy, and Experience which leads to philosophy, is as old as the world, disasters throwing up schorching deserts of sand in the field of thought arise from exclusive application to one or other of the two. Buddha's attempt was of this nature ; he severed philosophy from experience, and the fate of Buddhism after the Lord's *Nirvâṇa* amply attests the consequence.* S'ankara clearly understood this, and laying hold of the esoteric and exoteric *Vidyâ* spoken of in the *Upanishads* he effected an easy compromise between Philosophy and Experience, between Reason and Emotion, between Morality and Conduct, between Class and Class, between Society and Salvation. I know there are Orientalists denying this division of esoteric and exoteric knowledge in *Vedic* philosophy.† The distinction is, however,

* I am persuaded to believe there is no evidence to support the story of S'ankara inciting or ever working towards downright merciless massacre of Buddha's followers. The story bears evident marks of its being an invention of those who may not be in sympathy with the *Brâhmaṇic* revival under S'ankara. The causes of the decline of Buddhism lie, as I have tried to show, more within than without the Lord's teaching.

† Vide Prof. Max Muller's Psychological Religion; also Three Lectures on the *Vedânta* philosophy; etc. Certain writers of the so-called Reform-party in India think the *Vedânta* was a Protestant schism from the ideal of the *Veda*, and that their own new-fangled hobbles being protests of the same kind are, similarly, not beyond the pale of orthodox Hinduism. This involves a *false major*. There never was a Protest against Hinduism or the *Veda* save through Buddhism and Jainism. Even Vallabha and Ramânuja never led a schism. The former taught the Absolute Philosophy of S'ankara through Love, making way for devotion in place of gnosis and reflection. The latter materialized the Idea still further by imagining two Ideas in and out of a third, making way thus for pure objective worship and devotion. In either case they were more concessions to the requirements of the age, than protests of any kind.

clearly hinted at in the *parâ-* and *aparâ- vidyâ*, in the *para-* and *apara- Brahman* of many an *Upanishad*-text. And but for this distinction the philosophy of S'ankara, perhaps all philosophy whatever, had no ground to stand upon. Unless experience were a school of wisdom, leading to graduation in that which is beyond experience, there were no sense in talking of Philosophy or of the ultimate truth of things. S'ankara emphasised this distinction and showed the value of experience, the use of formal religion and objective worship, the necessity of distinction in unity, the truth of one in many. Without at all tarnishing the glory of the high aspiration of this Philosophy, he re-established in full fresh vigour the ancient ideal in the heart of the nation, pointed out the way to supreme peace while yet in the world, and left to posterity an unfailing source of the most sublime synthesis of philosophy, morals, religion and experience.

Too much of exotericism ends in rigid formalism, in a life savouring too much of the sweet world and its fashionable ways. Exclusive attention to the esoteric tends to the wordy vagueness of metaphisyes or the jugglery of low magic and equally degrading spiritualism. When all exoteric forms of life and living, religion and science, are seen and experienced through the esoteric Idea; when, in short, the whole variety of experience (including all the known fields of human activity) is looked upon as so many grades of a course of training leading ultimately to the Idea which is ever going out of and returning into itself at every step and in very being; the reconciliation of exoteric and esoteric is complete in the inexpressible unity of Truth. In this consists the practical value of Absolute Idealism. Twelve years back, I remember to have given a paradoxical sub-title to my small book on the *Râja-Yoga*; I called it 'Practical Metaphysics of the *Vedânta*.' Subsequent study has confirmed the conviction which thus expressed itself at the time. In the mode of thought we are considering philosophy cannot sever itself from science, morals from religion, spirit from life, the Idea from the fact, reason from emotion. Education, Art, Politics, Society, Family—none of the interests of humanity—can ever be considered apart from the Idea which they must each and all embody and express, approach and imitate, realize and retain. Lay hold of the Idea and by a process of deduction descend to any particular you desire. This philosophy is the philosophy of Universals. It does not begin with particulars to end again in some confounding particular, it descends from the universal to the particular.

Every atom is thus at once a universe to itself. It finds the particular of its being from the universal it embodies and lives up to. Not an act, not a thought, not a single ruffle of human atmosphere is here present in vain, no chance rules Nature, nothing ever remains in a state of permanent equilibrium, nothing continues ever to move. Equilibrium and motion is the constant law of Recompense which, in a moment, in a single flight of Imagination, in one life or many lives, repairs the apparent wrong of every being, preserves and conserves every energy expended apparently in a fruitless idle manner on any plane whatever. Every being thus realizes the Idea in and through the Fact; in and through life and experience bound up with life. There is no private sanctum or public church where you can weep over your woes or sing your repentence into the ears of some merciful Being. Every atom carries its sanctum and its church within itself, in the Idea which it embodies, in the Fact which it is :— in the realization it has at any moment gained of this its real Self, through the fact it is. The Fact ever drags it away from the Unit, the Idea lifts it to It ; this happens daily, hourly, every moment. And according as the God one obeys does he find the meed of his act in the course of time.

'Live in and through the Idea, yield not to the Fact, the external exoteric shell of eternal Thought,' this has been the moral standard of this Philosophy. 'Look upon every being as upon your Self' says an Indian book of children's precepts. The calm equation of peaceful being thus found in busy, active life and its absorbing interests, is but another statement of the law of the conservation of spiritual energy. Work and be not affected with the work or its result ; use your-self without feeling the friction of use ;—this comes of realizing the Idea. Asceticism is not at all the moral or religious Ideal of this philosophy. It is a philosophy of action, of straight active performance of duty, of pure disinterested honest love. The madness which intoxicates any two individuals with the sweetness of reciprocal presence is the least of that Love which is the very God of this philosophy, so to speak Full vision of the Idea, realization of one-ness with the Idea expressing itself in any and every *fact* ; the universal, transcendent sense of that passive self-gratulating complascence or quiet through which every individual is ever in love with itself ; may be described as that Love which is the Gospel of this Philosophy. Forsake not this equanimity of one-ness with the Idea, whatever its form or expression, do your duty as duty is understood on the plane you are acting, and the Eternal Law shall never disturb you in the peace of silent bliss called Liberation or *Kaivalya.* The Idea is for ever liberated. If the *forms* of the Idea cease to entice and delude away from Itself, liberation is at once realized, the Idea at once gains itself, the process of self-realization is complete. 'Fulfil the law of thy nature, take no concern of the result' has been the burden of Kṛshṇa's Revelation to his dear friend and pupil Arjuna. S'ankara and his followers preached their Philosophy to the same end.

Thus it was the strength of this Idea that supported Harischandra who, abandoning a wealthy and prosperous kingdom, sold his wife, child and finally himself for the fulfilment of a promise, made in dream. Thus did Râma tear himself away, without a pang, from his innocent sweetheart, lest through his person may reach some blemish to the ideal of his race and king-dom. Thus did Arjuna fight thousands of his friends and relatives on the field of Kurukshetra in obedience to the call of duty ; thus Kṛshṇa, ever busy in a variety of ways, remains an ascetic, the one God of the Indian Nation. Thus did Pratâpa and S'ivâji or heroic women like the queen of

Jhansi yet in her teens fight the battles of Hinduism; thus did the Rajaput race earn glory in sacrificing themselves at a moment's call to the cause of their country and religion. Life in India is permeated through and through with the leaven of this Idea. In modern 'civilized' times we look at it from the wrong end, and find everything amiss. Instead of grasping the Deductive Universal and descending from it to particulars, we begin with the Inductive particular and end in confusion, misunderstanding, and abuse.

And the main principle of the Absolute Philosophy is not as absurd or difficult as it is often misunderstood to be. Nor is it philosophy for the few, for the study; the poorest intellect can understand it, the most fashionable drawing-room may be enlivened with it. It requires only the eye to read the Idea, so to speak, into every act, every word, every thought; into every thing, every experience. Not that you learn some new chemistry which will place you in possession of the 'Universal solvent' or bring you a reality of the Alchemist's dream. You only get the eye which opens to a higher Chemistry, a higher Science. The Philosopher's stone and the immortal Elixir are in your possession, for you now realise the immensity of law, the silent wonder of infinite knowledge, the distinctionless unity of life and love.

Every one is perfectly sure of his 'Self' and of the love and duty he owes to his 'Self.' This philosophy only requires that this love and this duty be extended to embrace all 'selves' in one 'Self.' The wildest boor in India understands this, the most fastidious of the country values this, every aged male or female devotes the remaining part of life to contemplation of this. We may try to explain this central idea in a few words. S'ankara bases his Idealism on the undeniable evidence of individual consciousness. The consciousness which is the self of one is the same throughout all selves;* what differs is the *form*, the outer manifestation of inner consciousness. This pure consciousness is called *Sat*

* Every nameable thing is described as a self in this philosophy.

(Being), *Brahman* (the All), *Âtman* (Self), *Bhumâ* (the Unconditioned) and so on; in truth, It is the Unnameable, the Inexpressible, the one Residuum after negation of every position. This formless, immaterial consciousness is the one fact of all phenomena, it is, in fact, an abstract, a synthesis, of all being; or, more adequately still, it is only a name to express the sum total of all possible individual units in what we call the limitless kosmos. Every manifestation is a manifestation of this Idea; the world of experience is only the form the Idea takes in going out of itself to return again into itself. This going out of and returning into itself is the very being of the Idea, and the peace of its realization is between this efflux and influx, the daily, hourly law of all existence and activity. 'He who stands firm whatever may come or go' is the real knower of *Brahman*. The state of this place of peace between action and inaction, between life and death, between being and non-being, is simply indescribable, inexpressible. Find this *fulcrum*, and you have got the Archemedian lever which can lift the globe of this earth.

The Idea must be realized to be understood, whence it is usually described as self-realizable, and the bliss itself is often called self-realization. Knowing and being, knowledge and belief, go hand in hand, are one in that Unit whose only expression is the speech of Silence. From this nature of the Idea it is evident that all manifestation is so much illusion. It is illusion in that it draws the Self away from the Idea which only appears or re-appears as the phenomenon. Thus it is not difficult to understand how every Self has its own world, how it can make or unmake this world. This is matter of daily experience. There are as many worlds within worlds as there are beings in what we know as the World. No effort of language, no stretch of imagination can embrace the whole world under some common description. Every being has its World large or small, rich or poor, pleasant or sorrowful, light or dark, according as it chooses to make it. And the same applies to what passes for Duty, Morality, Honour, Learning, etc., in this imaginary world. One awakened to the Idea sees it all like a ladder on which the Self slowly climbs to self-realization, extending its vision at every turn, gaining itself with every ascent, and approaching the in-expressible silence of seeing itself in every Self as it nears the giddy top. Thus is the world an illusion out and out.

With the Idea running out on lines of manifestation are presupposed the necessary conditions of all manifestation whatever. Time, space, causality is all that is meant by manifestation, the Idea as soon as you conceive it as *becoming* presupposes these three which do not exist in the Unit. The phenomenal world is an illusion of these three forms, and all that belongs to the phenomenal is therefore subject to the law of Necesity. The cause-less, time-less, space-less Idea beyond Illusion is ever free. It is free to create or destroy its own world, to work its way to self-realization or to wait awhile on any rung of the ladder of experience which leads to self-realization.

And even happiness or bliss is for ever centred in self-realization. Every being feels happy or otherwise on finding or not finding a reflection of himself. He always desires what is in him, loves what is loveable in him, and feels happy on finding his ideal, his Self, in whatever seems to please him. He is free to enlarge the idea of his 'self' up to the inexpressible universal Idea. All misery, fear, doubt, narrowness are born of his imagination. Realization of the Self within him as one with the Idea is the real aim and object of existence. For until this is done, no peace is found in the forms of *Prakṛti* (illusive matter) which bind the Idea and create that variety of thoughts, feelings, likes and dislikes which ever interferes with the peace and well-being of the world. The highest moral good is Self-realization to which end experience, illusion though it is, provides the necessary training. Empty your 'self' of all contents whatever, run it beyond all possible limits, raise it above all kinds of relation;—thus through experience gain that education which leads to the realization of the Idea.* It is there your pulse beats with the pulse of nature, your heart responds to the heart of the Universe, and you find yourself in all and all in yourself. "Then has he access to all worlds, he has gained the empire of self."† Uddâlaka taught his impertinent son puffed up with the exoteric learning he had acquired, that esoteric truth whereby knowledge of One can lead to knowledge of all. The one Idea being realized as present throughout nature, every being is realized as one's own Self. Action is deprived of its sting of jealousy and hate. The Self then melts, indeed, as a lump of salt in the sea, never again to be regained, as the *Bṛhadâraṇyaka* puts it. The bliss which accompanies the eye that perceives the Idea through every fact and being, every thought and act, is simply indescribable, immeasurable, infinite. If we experience some abrupt yet agreeable tickling of momentary surprise even at ordinary sleight-of-hand magic what deep silence must surround the blissful wonder of that Magic which disillusions you into the indescribable one-ness of the All.

And the means to this realization is *reflection* and *reflection* alone. The forms of religion, the physical exercises of *Yoga*, point to the aspirant yet unable to realize the Ideal, the way to reflection and gnosis. Reflection reveals the Truth at a mere hint, through a casual remark, from a chance expression, by sympathetic awakening from the words of some book or teacher: 'Thou art That.' 'You become what you think,' says Yâjnavalkya. In the pure heart is reflected the spirit of the All, and the Enlightened henceforward forgets even the fact of his having become

---

* Readers of Philosophic literature will like to be told that what Schopenhauer calls the Will has here been described as the Idea and its synonyms. What he calls Idea is called form, manifestation, Illusion of the Idea. Though the Idealism here expounded agrees largely with Kantean modes of thought, his fiction of a thing-in-itself is here consigned to the oblivion it deserves. Hegel's Absolute Philosophy is not quite out of mind in this presentation of the same phase of thought.

† Bṛhadâraṇyaka.

the Light. He acts without concert, without premeditation, without hesitation or doubt. 'He lives the present out with smiling heart, taking no thought of the future or of the past' says Vasishtha to his beloved pupil Râma. In doubt and fear is the death of all philosophy, all high aim, all disinterested morals. Scepticism never yet created one single grain of sand for the innumerable gorgeous edifices it demolished. 'The ignorant and sceptic meet with certain destruction' says Shri Kṛshṇa; and in the absence of all intellectual doubt is the test of the last initiation into the *sanctum sanctorum* of this Philosophy of *Brahman*.

In a popular work of this kind this brief outline of the principal points of S'ankara's philosophy is sufficient to prepare the reader for due appreciation of what follows. Curious readers will elsewhere find more on the same subject. I have tried to divest the subject of its *S'âstric* garb; and much as some pedants may grudge the liberty thus taken, I for one would consider it a serious misfortune for the *Advaita* if it had to be dressed up in its peculiar garb to be presentable or distinguishable in the light of present-day thought. It is these pedants who "always at their best while talking of *Brahman*" as S'ankara puts it, are "without the heart having at all *become* It," that have brought the Absolute Philosophy into disrepute by encumbering it with words from which the spirit of love and compassion, the spirit of universality and equality, has been parched up in its passage through the scorching desert of their heart. S'ankara preached universal love, active honest work, constant repose in the peace and silence of the Idea.

This philosophy and the manner in which S'ankara applied it to the situation of his time, has been the true saviour of India. It is destined to be the saviour of the world. If the sympathetic reader has gathered enough from this brief introduction to interpret, assimilate and apply the ideas contained in the following pages, I have every confidence he will never part from this collection, he will certainly set apart a quiet morning or evening hour to its grave contemplation every day. It has been so with me, and the immense benefit this reading has done me is my only excuse in thus earnestly inviting my fellow-men to this elevating study.

NADIAD:
Vijayâdas'ami, 1951.
28th September 1895.

MANILAL. N. DVIVEDI.

ERRATA.

Page	*Line*	*Incorrect*	*Correct*
1	12	self	pelf
6	13	XII-XIII	XXII-XXIII
21	13–14	it, its	he, his
35	2	CXXIV	i—Reasoning CXXIV
36	12	CXXIX-CXXXI	ii—Learning CXXIX-CXXXI
48	4	*thinking*	*reflection*
53	14	beyond decay,	beyond sin, decay,
63	13	From him	From Him
72	11	beloves	behoves
79	3	on the Idea	on to the Idea
79	12–13	A collection of water is not all that makes a holy place, a lump of earth or stone is not all that makes a God ;	Not the collection of water that makes a holy place, not the lump of earth or stone that makes a God ;
89	8	CCXCVIX	CCXCIX
104	9	spike into its	spike of sorrow into its
132	6	ourself ;	our-self ;
136	19	on	or
140	3	lethargy ?	lethargy ;
141	18	*Bhâgavadgitá*	*Bhagavadgitâ*
149	13	it self	it-self
168	3	If of he	If he
168	5	anxitey	anxiety
183	7	fluses	flushes

शुद्धिपत्रम्

पृष्ठम्	पङ्क्तिः	अशुद्धम्	शुद्धम्
९	२६	दृष्टे	द्दष्टे
११	१७	नृ शाला...पः भुं	नृत्यशाला...पः प्रभुं
१५	२५	द्रष्टृ	द्रष्ट्र
३३	२४	यस्तृदा	यस्तूदा
४८	२७	भगवे	भगवो
७५	२५	एयमेव	एवमेव
८७	२९	जीवन्मुक्तिविवेकेः	जीवन्मुक्तिविवेके.
९६	२२	परमोपरीर्तांह	परमोपरातिर्हि
१७५	१६	साख्यं	साङ्ख्यं
१७६	२९	स्वराज्यासिद्धिः	स्वाराज्यसिद्धिः
१९७	२२	वेदविदांवर	वेद्यविदांवर

THE IMITATION OF S'ANKARA.

(*Being a collection of numerous texts on the Advaita.*)

I.—THE PROLOGUE.

I.

THAT wherein disappears the whole of that which affects the mind, and that which is also the background of all;—to that Self I bow,—all eternal consciousness, the witness of all *forms* of the Intellect.*

Upadeśasâhasri.

II.

MANY indeed are the teachers who appease themselves with the Self of their pupils; I lay myself prostrate before S'ankara who alone allays many a heart-burning of those who betake themselves to him.†

Miscellaneous.

---

* येनात्मना विलीयन्त उद्भवन्ति च वृत्तयः ।
नित्यावगतये तस्मै नमो धीप्रत्ययात्मने ॥

उपदेशसाहस्री.

† गुरवो बहवः सन्ति शिष्यवित्तापहारिणः ।
तमेकं शङ्करं वन्दे शिष्यसन्तापहारिणम् ॥

प्रास्ताविकः

III.

I expound in half a verse what has been told in a million volumes ;—*Brahman* is the Truth, the world is illusion, the soul is none other than *Brahman*.*

Miscellaneous.

IV—VIII.

ACTION leads to incarnation, and incarnation to pleasure and pain. Hence arise all likes and dislikes which again propel to action resulting in religious merit and demerit. These put the ignorant wanderer, again, into the bonds of incarnation ;—and so on and on, for ever, rolls the wheel of this world. Nothing but ignorance is the cause of all this ; the remedy lies in the destruction of ignorance. Knowledge of *Brahman* is the way to find final beatitude in the destruction of this ignorance, for knowledge alone, not action which is only a part of ignorance, is competent to accomplish this result. Nor is it possible to do away with likes and dislikes as long as ignorance is not done away with. This is therefore undertaken with the object of destroying ignorance as well as its effect—this world,—and also of explaining the real philosophy of *Brahman*.†

Upades'asâhasri.

---

* श्लोकार्धेन प्रवक्ष्यामि यदुक्तं ग्रन्थकोटिभिः ।
ब्रह्म सत्यं जगन्मिथ्या जीवो ब्रह्मैव नापरः ॥

प्रास्ताविकः

† कर्माणि देहयोगार्थं देहयोगे प्रियाप्रिये ।
ध्रुवे स्यातां ततो रागो द्वेषश्चैव ततः क्रियाः ॥
धर्माधर्मौ ततोऽज्ञस्य देहयोगस्तथा पुनः ।
एवं नित्यप्रवृत्तोऽयं संसारश्चक्रवद्भृशं ॥
अज्ञानं तस्य मूलं स्यादिति तद्धानमिष्यते ।
ब्रह्मविद्यात आरब्धा ततो निश्रेयसं भवेत् ॥
विद्यैवाज्ञानहानाय न कर्माप्रतिकूलतः ।
नाज्ञानस्याप्रहाणे हि रागद्वेषक्षयो भवेत् ॥
तस्मादज्ञानहानाय संसारविनिवृत्तये ।
ब्रह्मविद्याविधानाय प्रारब्धोपनिषत्त्वियं ॥

उपदेशसाहस्री.

IX—XII.

FROM the senses finding each its own gratification in the objects peculiar to each, there arises no real happiness but only a temporary allaying of the heat of the mind. It is vain, therefore, to grope for any real happiness in the world of objects. The deluded deceive themselves by imagining every dose of evil to be so much good; but in birth, death, and limitedness, the wise never fail to perceive the evil that conceals itself under the inviting form of objects. They find no happiness in things subject to such results. The smallest happiness, in the real sense of the word, is nohow possible in any thing;—oh! I should become that Self which is all bliss, all existence, all enlightenment.*

Âtmapurâṇa.

XIII.

KNOWLEDGE of the Divine dissolves all bonds, and gives freedom from every kind of misery including birth and death.†

S'vetâśvataropanishad.

---

* एवं शब्दादिलाभेऽपि सुखं नैव प्रजायते ।
किन्तु स्वात्मन औत्सुक्यनिवृत्तिः स्यात्क्षणं नृणाम् ॥
ततो न जायते किञ्चित्सुखं विषयतो नृणाम् ।
किन्तु दुःखेषु सुखधीः क्रियते भ्रान्तबुद्धिभिः ॥
जनिनाशाल्पतायाश्च दोषा विषयजा नृणाम् ।
फले तस्मिन् कथं नाम सुखधीर्धीमतो भवेत् ॥
ततो न जायते किञ्चित् सुखं क्वापि कथञ्चन ।
आनन्दात्मा ततोऽहं स्यां सत्प्रकाशैकरूपवान् ॥

आत्मपुराणम्.

† ज्ञात्वा देवं सर्वपाशापहानिः । क्षीणैः क्लेशैर्जन्ममृत्युप्रहाणिः ॥

श्वेताश्वतरोपनिषत्.

XIV.

THE Creator (*Brahmâ*), the Protector (*Vishṇu*), the Destroyer (*Rudra*), the Consumer (*agni*)), the Sun, the Moon, the Thunderer (*Indra*), the Wind (*Marut*), the Sacrifice, and so on, the sages describe the One eternal Ens, as they look at it through the multifarious forms of the intellect ;—all my best worship to that Divine Essence, the destroyer of that ignorance whose form is this world.*

S'ankarâchârya.

II.—BRAHMAN.

XV—XVI.

THAT should be known as *Brahman* beyond the gaining whereof there remains nothing to gain, beyond the bliss whereof there remains no possibility of bliss, beyond the sight whereof there remains nothing to see, beyond becoming which there remains nothing to become, beyond knowing which there remains nothing to know.†

Âtmabodha.

---

* ब्रह्मा विष्णू रुद्रहुताशौ रविचंद्रा
विंद्रो वायुर्यज्ञ इतीत्थं परिकल्प्य ।
एकं संतं यं बहुधाहुर्मतिभेदा
त्तं संसारध्वान्तविनाशं हरिमीडे ॥

हरिमीडेस्तोत्रम्.

† यल्लाभान्नापरो लाभो यत्सुखान्नापरं सुखं ।
यज्ज्ञानान्नापरं ज्ञानं तद्ब्रह्मेत्यवधारयेत् ॥
यद्दृष्ट्वान्नापरं दृश्यं यद्भूत्वा न पुनर्भवः ।
यज्ज्ञात्वा न परं ज्ञेयं तद्ब्रह्मेत्यवधारयेत् ॥

आत्मबोध.

XVII.

THIS is full, and so is that ;—full comes out of the full,—taking away the full from the full, the full remains for ever.*

I'sopanishad.

XVIII.

HE is eternal among the eternal, conscious among the conscious ; He, ever one, produces the variety of ideas in the many ;—knowing that Divine One, realizable by *Sânkhya* or *Yoga*, as the Supreme Cause, all bonds dissolve themselves into nothing.†

S'vetâśvataropanishad.

XIX.

HE who, in the beginning, sent forth the Creator (*Brahmâ*) and favoured him with the storehouse of all knowledge, the *Veda* ;—I, desirous of liberation, betake myself to Him, the ever-effulgent light, revealing his eternal Self through the intellect.‡

S'vetáśvataropanishad.

---

* पूर्णमदः पूर्णमिदं पूर्णात्पूर्णमुदच्यते ।
पूर्णस्य पूर्णमादाय पूर्णमेवावशिष्यते ॥

ईशोपनिषत्.

† नित्यो नित्यानां चेतनश्चेतताना
मेको बहूनां योविदधाति कामान् ।
तत्कारणं साङ्ख्ययोगाधिगम्यं
ज्ञात्वा देवं मुच्यते सर्वपाशैः ॥

श्वेताश्वतरोपनिषत्.

‡ यो ब्रह्माणं विदधाति पूर्वं यो वै वेदांश्च प्रहिणोति तस्मै ।
तं ह देवमात्मबुद्धिप्रकाशं मुमुक्षुर्वै शरणं प्रपद्ये ॥

श्वेताश्वतरोपनिषत्.

XX.

AS in the sun, all light, there is neither day nor night, so in the Self, all light, their is neither knowledge nor ignorance.*

Upadeśasâhasri.

XXI.

THE ever unchangeable is devoid of sound, touch, form, taste or smell. It is without beginning or end, ever beyond the prime cause of all evolution (*viz.*, the *Mahat*);—knowing that, one escapes the all-devouring jaws of death.†

Kathopanishad.

XII—XIII.

THE eye has no access there, nor has speech nor mind ; we do not know It (the Self), nor the method whereby we can impart It. It is other than the known as well as the unknown ; so indeed do we hear from the sages of old who explained It thus to us.‡

Kenopanishad.

---

* नाहोरात्रे यथासूर्ये प्रभारूपाविशेषतः ।
बोधरूपाविशेषान्न बोधाबोधौ तथात्मनि ॥

उपदेशसाहस्री.

† अशब्दमस्पर्शमरूपमव्ययं तथारसन्नित्यमगन्धवच्च यत् ।
अनाद्यनन्तम्महतः परन्ध्रुवं निचाय्य तन्मृत्युमुखात्प्रमुच्यते ॥

कठोपनिषद्.

‡ न तत्र चक्षुर्गच्छति नवाग्गच्छति नामनो ।
न विद्मो न विजानीमोयथैतदनुशिष्यात् ॥
अन्यदेव तद्विदितादथोविदितादधि ।
इति शुश्रुम पूर्वेषां ये नस्तद्व्याचचक्षिरे ॥

केनोपनिषद्.

XXIV.

TRY to realise (within thyself) that whence arise these beings, by which they stand sustained, and unto which they return and become naught ;—that indeed is *Brahman.* *

Taittiriyopanishad.

XXV—XXVI.

TO the emperor (Janaka) thus explained Yâjnavalkya;—When there is, *as it were*, a second, there alone does one see, smell or taste somethig other (than Self), there alone does one speak to or hear, think of or touch or know something other (than Self) ;—but when the seer is all alone by himself, he is as still as an undisturbed collection of water,—this indeed is *Brahmaloka*, the condition of universal empire. This to the self, is the highest end, the best riches, the supremest world, the greatest joy ;—the rest of beings live only by a particle of this bliss.†

Bṛhadâraṇyakopanishad.

---

* यतोवा इमानि भूतानि जायन्ते येन जातानि जीवन्ति यत्प्रयन्त्याभिसंविशन्ति तद्विजिज्ञासस्व । तद्ब्रह्म ॥

तैत्तिरीयोपनिषन्.

† यत्रवाऽन्यदिव स्यात्तत्राऽन्योऽन्यत्पश्येदन्योऽन्यजिघ्रेदन्योऽन्यद्रसयेदन्योऽन्यद्वदेदन्योऽन्यच्छृणुयादन्योऽन्यन्मन्वीतान्योऽन्यत्स्पृशेदन्योऽन्यद्विजानीयात् ॥

सलिलएकोद्रष्टाद्वैतोभवत्येष ब्रह्मलोकः सम्राडितिहैनमनुशशास याज्ञवल्क्य एषास्य परमागतिरेषास्यपरमा सम्पदेषोऽस्य परमोलोक एषोऽस्यपरमआनन्द एतस्यैवानन्दस्यान्यानिभूतानि मात्रामुपजीवन्ति ॥

बृहदारण्यकोपनिषत्.

XXVII—XXVIII.

FATHER, son, mother, nay even the worlds, the Gods, the *Vedas* are all naught in this (Self); the thief is no-thief, the fœticide no-fœticide, the *chândâla* no-*chândâla*, the *Poulkasa* no-*Poulkasa*, the *S'ramaṇa* no-*S'ramaṇa*, the ascetic no-ascetic; —It has no relation with good or evil. One who has become It is beyond all desires of the heart. It should not be supposed that (even in sleep) It does not see, for It does not see though ever seeing; the sight of the seer is never lost, being eternal, there is nothing other than Itself which It can make the object of Its seeing.*

Bṛhadâraṇyakopanishad.

XXIX.

HENCE it is described as "not this," "not that," and so on by negatives only.†

Bṛhadârṇyakopanishad.

XXX.

THAT is real bliss which has no conditions; in the conditioned there can be no happiness;—the Unconditioned alone is bliss; try to realize the Unconditioned (in thyself.)‡

Chhândogyopanishad.

---

* अत्र पितापिताभवति मातामाता लोकाअलोका देवाअदेवा वेदाअवेदा अत्र स्तेनोऽस्तेनोभवति भ्रूणहाभ्रूणहा चाण्डालोऽचाण्डालः पौल्कसोऽपौल्कसः श्रमणोऽश्रमण स्तापसोऽतापसोऽनन्वागतं पुण्येनानन्वागतं पापेन तीर्णो हि तदासर्वाञ्छोकान् हृदयस्यभवति ॥

यद्वै तन्नपश्यति पश्यन्नैतन्नपश्याति। न हि द्रष्टुर्दृष्टेर्विपरिलोपोविद्यतेऽविनाशित्वान्नतुतद्द्वितीयमस्ति ततोऽन्यद्विभक्तंयत्पश्येत् ॥

बृहदारण्यकोपनिषद्.

† अथात आदेशो नेतिनेतीति ॥

बृहदारण्यकोपनिषद्.

‡ यो वै भूमा तत्सुखं नाल्पे सुखमस्ति भूमैव सुखं भूमा त्वेव विजिज्ञासितव्यः ॥

छान्दोग्योपनिषत्.

XXXI.

THAT is the Unconditioned wherein one does not see another, one does not hear another, one does not know another; that wherein one sees another, hears another, knows another, is the conditioned. The Unconditioned is immortal, the conditioned is mortal. Oh master! where is this Unconditioned to be found? In its own glory, or even nowhere.*

Chhândogyopanishad.

XXXII.

HENCE is described the Self; Self alone stands above, below, west, east, south and north; everywhere all is Self. He who thus sees, thinks and knows, enjoys Self, plays with Self, has Self alone even for a second, finds perfect bliss in Self, becomes the lord of all, gains access to all worlds and beings. Those who understand otherwise, betake themselves to other masters, enjoy only the mortal world of conditions, find no access to all beings and all worlds.†

Chhândogyopanishad.

---

* यत्र नान्यत्पश्यति नान्यच्छृणोति नान्यद्विजानाति स भूमा अथ यत्रान्यत्पश्यत्यन्यच्छृणोत्यन्यद्विजानाति तदल्पं यो वै भूमा तदमृतमथ यदल्पं तन्मर्त्यं स भगवः कस्मिन् प्रतिष्ठित इति स्वे महिम्नि यदि वा न महिम्नीति ॥

छान्दोग्योपनिषत्.

† अथात आत्मादेश एवात्मैवाधस्तादात्मोपरिष्टादात्मा पश्चादात्मा पुरस्तादात्मा दक्षिणत आत्मोत्तरत आत्मैवेदं सर्वमिति स वा एष एवं पश्यन्नेवं मन्वान एवं विजानन्नात्मरतिरात्मक्रीड आत्ममिथुन आत्मानन्दः स स्वराड्भवति तस्य सर्वेषु लोकेषु कामचारो भवति अथ येऽन्यथाऽतो विदुरन्यराजानस्ते क्षय्यलोका भवन्ति तेषां सर्वेषु लोकेष्वकामचारो भवति ॥

छान्दोग्योपनिषत्.

XXXIII—XXXV.

THAT soul which is ever awake even in sleep, sending forth the variety of ideas, is said to be all pure *Brahman*, all immortality ;—all the worlds are held in it (as it were, in suspension), there is nothing which transcends it. It is this. As the *one* fire pervading the universe *appears* in so many forms in the variety of objects, so the inner self of all, ever one, appears to take on so many forms, but is ever beyond them. As the sun who enlightens everything has nothing whatever to do with the numerous ills the eye may perceive, so the inner self of all, ever one, has no connection whatever with the joys and sorrows of the world, being ever beyond them.*

Kathopanishad.

XXXVI—XXXVIII.

THAT is the real witness (*viz.*, self), all consciousness, who unites in one grasp, the actor, act and the variety of objects apart one from the other. I see, hear, smell, taste and touch,—in this form does (the witness) unite all in one continuous consciousness, even like the lamp suspended in a theatre. The lamp in the theatre takes in the master, the audience, the actors and all, without distinction, in one sweep of light, and continues to shed the same light even when all these are not there.†

Panchadaśi.

---

* य एष सुप्तेषु जागर्ति कामं कामं पुरुषो निर्मिमाणः ।
तदेव शुक्रं तद्ब्रह्म तदेवामृतमुच्यते ।
तस्मिँल्लोकाः श्रिताः सर्वे तदु नात्येति कश्चन ॥ एतद्वैतत् ॥
अग्निर्यथैको भुवनं प्रविष्टो रूपं रूपं प्रतिरूपो बभूव ।
एकस्तथा सर्वभूतान्तरात्मा रूपं रूपं प्रतिरूपो बहिश्च ॥
सूर्यो यथा सर्वलोकस्य चक्षुर्न लिप्यते चाक्षुषैर्बाह्यदोषैः ।
एकस्तथा सर्वभूतान्तरात्मा न लिप्यते लोकदुःखेन बाह्यः ॥

कठोपनिषत्.

† कर्तारं च क्रियां तद्वद्व्यावृत्तविषयानपि ।
स्फोरयेदेकयत्नेन योऽसौ साक्ष्यत्र चिद्वपुः ॥

XXXIX.

THE seer of thy sight thou shalt not see, the hearer of thy ear thou shalt not hear, the thinker of thy thoughts thou shalt not think, the knower of thy knowledge thou shalt not know—this is thy Sẹlf, all-pervading, everything besides is but mortal.*

Bṛhadâraṇyakopanishad.

XL.

WITHOUT the glass there is no possibility of a sight of the reflection; whence then could there be any possibility of the knowledge of *name* and *forms* without assuming that which is existence, consciousness, and bliss? †

Panchadaśi.

ईक्षे शृणोमि जिघ्रामि स्वादयामि स्पृशाम्यहम् ।
इति भासयते सर्वं नृत्यशालास्थदीपवत् ॥
नृत्यशालास्थितो दीपः प्रभुं सभ्यांश्च नर्तकीम् ।
दीपयेदविशेषेण तदभावेऽपि दीप्यते ॥

पञ्चदशी.

* न दृष्टेर्द्रष्टारं पश्येर्न श्रुतेःश्रोतारं शृणुया न मतेर्मन्तारं मन्वीथा न विज्ञाते-र्विज्ञातारं विजानीथा एष त आत्मा सर्वान्तरोऽतोऽन्यदार्तम् ॥

बृहदारण्यकोपनिषत्.

† अदृष्ट्वा दर्पणं नैव तदन्तस्थेक्षणं तथा ।
अमत्वा सच्चिदानंदं नामरूपमतिः कुतः ॥

पञ्चदशी.

XLI—XLIII.

HE pervades the earth and yet transcends it; the earth knows Him not; the earth is His body: He controls the earth from within;—He is thy inner Self ever immortal. He pervades water and yet transcends it; water knows Him not; water is His body: He controls water from within;—He is thy inner Self ever immortal. * * * * * He is the unseen seer, the unheard hearer, the unthought thinker, the unknown knower; there is no seer other than this, no hearer other than this, no thinker other than this, no knower other than this;—this is thy (and of all beings') inner self, ever immortal; all beside is mortal.†

Brhadâranyakopanishad.

XLIV—XLVIII.

THAT which is not spoken in speech but that whereby all speech is spoken; that which does not think in the mind but that whereby the mind proceeds to think; that which does not perceive with the eye but that whereby the eye receives its sight; that which does not hear with the ear but that whereby the ear hears; that which does not breathe the breath

---

* The same is said of fire, air, wind, heaven, sun, moon, stars, light, darkness, space, skin, speech, eyes, ears, mind, breath,—all beings whatever.

† यःपृथिव्यां तिष्ठन् पृथिव्या अन्तरोयं पृथिवी न वेद यस्य पृथिवी शरीरं यः पृथिवीमन्तरो यमयत्येष त आत्मान्तर्याम्यमृतः ॥

योऽप्सु तिष्ठन्नपोऽन्तरोयमापोन विदुर्यस्यापः शरीरं योऽपोन्तरो यमयत्येष त आत्मान्तर्याम्यमृतः ॥

अदृष्टोद्रष्टाऽश्रुतः श्रोतामतोमन्ताविज्ञातो विज्ञाता नान्योऽतोऽस्ति द्रष्टा नान्योऽतोऽस्ति श्रोता नान्योऽतोऽस्ति मन्ता नान्योऽतोऽस्ति विज्ञातैष त आत्मान्तर्याम्यमृतोऽतोऽन्यदार्तम् ॥

बृहदारण्यकोपनिषत्.

of life but that whereby life itself is kept up ;—Know thou that that is *Brahman*, not this that people worship.*

Kenopanishad.

XLIX.

IMMORTAL *Brahman* alone is all this ; the east, west, south and north is all *Brahman* ; this wide expanse of the universe above and below is indeed all *Brahman*.†

Muṇdakopanishad.

L.

IN the beginning, oh good one! was the Ens alone ; all one without a second.‡

Chhândagyopanishad.

---

* यद्वाचानभ्युदितं येन वागभ्युद्यते ।
तदेव ब्रह्म त्वं विद्धि नेदं यदिदमुपासते ॥
यन्मनसा न मनुते येनाहुर्मनो मतम् ।
तदेव ब्रह्म त्वं विद्धि नेदं यदिदमुपासते ॥
यच्चक्षुषा न पश्यति येन चक्षूंषि पश्यति ।
तदेव ब्रह्म त्वं विद्धि नेदं यदिदमुपासते ॥
यच्छ्रोत्रेण न शृणोति येन श्रोत्रमिदं श्रुतम् ।
तदेव ब्रह्म त्वं विद्धि नेदं यदिदमुपासते ॥
यत्प्राणेन न प्राणिति येन प्राणः प्रणीयते ।
तदेव ब्रह्म त्वं विद्धि नेदं यदिदमुपासते ॥

केनोपनिषत्.

† ब्रह्मैवेदममृतं पुरस्ताद्ब्रह्म पश्चाद्ब्रह्म दक्षिणतश्चोत्तरेण ।
अधश्चोर्ध्वञ्च प्रसृतं ब्रह्मैवेदं विश्वमिदं वरिष्ठम् ॥

मुण्डकोपनिषत्.

‡ सदेव सौम्येदमग्र आसीदेकमेवाद्वितीयम् ।

छान्दोग्योपनिषत्.

LI.

BRAHMÂ, Indra, Prajâpati, all the gods, the five primordial elements, and all that breathes, or moves about, or flies above, or stands unmoved,—the whole (universe) exists through Thought, depends on Thought, Thought is its stay ;—Thought is *Brahman.**

Aitareyopanishad.

LII.

THIS self—*Brahman*—is all intellect, all mind, all life, all eyes, all ears, all earth, all water, all wind, all ether, all light, all darkness, all desires, all peacefulness, all anger, all quiet, all religious merit, all religious demerit ; It is the All, It is this, It is that.†

Bṛhadâraṇyakopanishad.

LIII.

THIS *Brahman* is causeless, without a second, having no within and without ; this self is *Brahman*, the consciousness of all.‡

Bṛhadáraṇyakopanishad.

---

* एष ब्रह्मैष इन्द्र एष प्रजापतिरेते सर्वे देवा इमानि च पञ्चमहाभूतानि * * * यत्किञ्चेदं प्राणिजङ्गमं च पतत्रि च यच्च स्थावरं सर्वं तत्प्रज्ञानेत्रं प्रज्ञाने प्रतिष्ठितं प्रज्ञा प्रतिष्ठा प्रज्ञानं ब्रह्म ॥

ऐतरेयोपनिषत्.

† स वा अयमात्मा ब्रह्म विज्ञानमयो मनोमयः प्राणमयश्चक्षुर्मयः श्रोत्रमयः पृथ्वीमय आपोमयो वायुमय आकाशमयस्तेजोमयोऽतेजोमयः काममयोऽकाममयः क्रोधमयोऽक्रोधमयोधर्ममयोऽधर्ममयः सर्वमयस्तद्यदेतदिदम्मयोऽदोमय इति ॥

बृहदारण्यकोपनिषत्.

‡ तदेतद्ब्रह्मापूर्वमनपरमनन्तरमबाह्यमयमात्माब्रह्म सर्वानुभूः ॥

बृहदारण्यकोपनिषत्.

LIV.

OH Gârgi! this immutable one is the unseen Seer, the unheard Hearer, the unthought Thinker, the unknown, Knower;—there is no seer beside this, no hearer beside this, no thinker, no knower beside this. In this immutable (essence) oh dear Gàrgi! is interwoven the *âkâsa* (the last essence of all existence).*

Bṛhadâraṇyakopanishad.

LV.

HE (Yâjnavalkya) said oh Gârgi! the knowers of *Brahman* thus explain the ever Immutable. It is neither with dimensions nor atomic, neither short nor long; It is not red, not sticky, not light, not dark; neither air, nor ether. It has no relation, no taste, no smell, no eye, no ear, no speech, no mind, no light, no life, no mouth, no form, no break, no without;—It enjoys nothing or is enjoyed by nothing.†

Bṛhadâraṇyakopanishad.

LVI—LX.

I explain to thee that real thing, knowledge whereof confers immortal enjoyment;—It is supreme *Brahman* without beginning, beyond being as well as non-being. It is all hands, all feet, all eyes, all heads, all mouths, all ears. It stands embracing the whole universe within its ample fold. It illumines all

* तद्वा एतदक्षरं गार्ग्यदृष्टं द्रष्टृश्रुतं श्रोत्रमतं मन्त्रविज्ञातं विज्ञातृ नान्यदतोऽस्ति द्रष्टृ नाऽन्यदतोऽस्ति श्रोतृ नाऽन्यदतोऽस्ति मन्तृ नाऽन्यदतोऽस्ति विज्ञात्रेतस्मिन्नु खल्वक्षरे गार्ग्याकाश ओतश्चप्रोतश्चेति ॥

बृहदारण्यकोपनिषत्.

† स होवाचैतद्वैतदक्षरं गार्गि ब्राह्मणा अभिवदन्त्यस्थूलमनण्वह्रस्वमदीर्घमलोहितमस्नेहमच्छायमतमोऽवाय्वनाकाशमसङ्गमरसमगन्धमचक्षुष्कमश्रोत्रमवागमनोऽतेजस्कमप्राणममुखममात्रमनन्तरमबाह्यं न तदश्नाति किञ्चन न तदश्नाति कश्चन ॥

बृहदारण्यकोपनिषत्.

sensible objects though void of every sense, It sustains all though void of all relation, It reaps the fruition of all activity though void of every property ;—It is within and without all beings, It is immovable and yet ever moving, It is minutely unknowable, and yet constantly near though ever afar. Though ever unpartitioned It stands *as if* divided in all beings ; It is the sustainer, master and destroyer of all.*

Bhagvadgitâ.

LXI.—LXII.

OBJECTS transcend the senses, the mind transcends objects, the intellect transcends the mind, the *mahat* (*i.e.* cosmic intellection) transcends intellect (*i. e.* individual intellect), the *avyakta* (*i.e.* the undifferenced first cause), transcends the *mahat*, the *Purusha* (*i.e.* the Self) transcends the *avyakta*;—beyond the *Purusha* there is nothing which can transcend Him, or prevent Him from being the last essence, the last resort (of all).†

Kathopanishad.

---

* ज्ञेयं यत्तत्प्रवक्ष्यामि यज्ज्ञात्वामृतमश्नुते ।
अनादिमत्परं ब्रह्म न सत्तन्नासदुच्यते ॥
सर्वतः पाणिपादं तत्सर्वतोऽक्षिशिरोमुखम् ।
सर्वतः श्रुतिमल्लोके सर्वमावृत्य तिष्ठति ॥
सर्वेन्द्रियगुणाभासं सर्वेन्द्रियविवर्जितम् ।
असक्तं सर्वभृच्चैव निर्गुणं गुणभोक्तृ च ॥
बहिरन्तश्च भूतानामचरं चरमेव च ।
सूक्ष्मत्वात्तदविज्ञेयं दूरस्थं चान्तिके च तत् ॥
अविभक्तं च भूतेषु विभक्तमिव च स्थितम् ।
भूतभर्तृ च तज्ज्ञेयं ग्रसिष्णु प्रभविष्णु च ॥

भगवद्गीता.

† इन्द्रियेभ्यः परा ह्यर्था अर्थेभ्यश्च परं मनः ।
मनसस्तु परा बुद्धिर्बुद्धेरात्मा महान्परः ॥
महतः परमव्यक्तमव्यक्तात्पुरुषः परः ।
पुरुषान्न परं किञ्चित् सा काष्ठा सा परागतिः ॥

कठोपनिषत्.

LXIII.

THAT is the First Great *Purusha* who, though without hands or feet, is the swiftest of approach ; though without eyes or ears, sees and hears everything ; though uncomprehended, comprehends everything knowable.*

S'vetás'vataropanishad.

LXIV—LXVI.

THE all-seeing is never born, never dead ; It comes out of nothing or sends forth nothing ;—It is unborn, eternal, immutable, ever unique, never destroyed with the destruction of the body. If the killer intends to kill or if the killed thinks He is killed, both of them do not *know* ;—It neither kills nor is killed. It is smaller than an atom, greater than the greatest ; It is present in the heart of all beings. The glory of this Self is realized by him the whole of whose sensibility returns to a state of placid calmness through absence of desire ;—he alone passes to the other side of this ocean of sin and sorrow.†

Kathopanishad.

---

* अपाणिपादो जवनो ग्रहीता पश्यत्यचक्षुः स शृणोत्यकर्णः ।
स वेत्ति वेद्यं न च तस्याऽस्ति वेत्ता तमाहुरग्र्यं पुरुषं महान्तम्

श्वेताश्वतरोपनिषत्.

† न जायते म्रियते वा विपश्चिन्नायं कुतश्चिन्न बभूव कश्चित् ।
अजोनित्यः शाश्वतोऽयं पुराणो न हन्यते हन्यमाने शरीरे ॥
हन्ता चेन्मन्यते हन्तुं हतश्चेन्मन्यते हतम् ।
उभौ तौ न विजानीतो नायं हन्ति न हन्यते ॥
अणोरणीयान्महतोमहीयानात्मास्य जन्तोर्निहितो गुहायाम् ।
तमक्रतुः पश्यति वीतशोको धातुप्रसादान्महिमानमात्मनः ॥

कठोपनिषत्.

LXVII.—LXIX.

STEEL cuts It not, fire burns It not, water moistens It not, wind dries It not;—ever uncut, unburnt, unmoistened, undried, It is eternal, all-pervading, immovable, unchangeable; It is the All. It is said to be unmanifest, unthought, unalterable;—knowing It to be such thou needst not grieve.*

Bhagvadgitâ.

LXX.—LXXI.

TRUTH alone conquers, not falsehood, the divine path† stands upheld by Truth; sages with desires put out by satiety pass over it to the great treasure of Truth. It (the Truth) is all-embracing yet unthinkable, all light, minutest of the minute yet ever manifest. It is farthest of all yet ever near in all beings, ever present in the hidden consciousness of all which passes out in all acts (of mind and body). ‡

Mundakopanishad.

---

* नैनं छिन्दन्ति शस्त्राणि नैनं दहति पावकः ।
न चैनं क्लेदयन्त्यापो न शोषयति मारुतः ॥
अच्छेद्योऽयमदाह्योऽयमक्लेद्योऽशोष्य एव च ।
नित्यः सर्वगतः स्थाणुरचलोऽयं सनातनः ॥
अव्यक्तोऽयमचिन्त्योऽयमविकार्योऽयमुच्यते ।
तस्मादेवं विदित्वैनं नानुशोचितुमर्हसि ॥

भगवद्गीता.

† That is Devayàna the way by which the liberated pass through the sun to higher worlds and rest in absolute unity with all.

‡ सत्यमेव जयते नानृतं
सत्येन पन्था विततो देवयानः ।
येनाक्रमन्त्यृषयो ह्याप्तकामा
यत्र तत्सत्यस्य परमं निधानम् ॥
बृहच्चतद्दिव्यमचिन्त्यरूपं
सूक्ष्माच्चतत्सूक्ष्मतरं विभाति ।
दूरात्सुदूरे तदिहान्तिके च
पश्यत्स्विहैव निहितं गुहायाम् ॥

मुण्डकोपनिषत्.

LXXII.

ONE so freed from the bondage of senses transcends all material relation, and becoming all supreme light, regains his own Self. This indeed is Self. It is beyond mortality, beyond fear, It is Brahman ;—Truth is only another name of Brahman.*

Chhândogyopanishad.

LXXIII—LXXV.

THERE could hardly be any room for separateness in that intransmutable, formless, characterless, one Being which is beyond the relations of subject, object, instrument etc., which is every way full to the utmost like the waters surging above all things at the great cyclic deluge. In it merges the cause of illusion like darkness in light ;—there, verily, can be nothing like separateness in It, the highest essence, without character, and ever one without a second.†

Vivekachudámaṇi.

---

* अथ य एष सम्प्रसादोऽस्माच्छरीरात्समुत्थाय परं ज्योतिरुपसम्पद्य स्वेन रूपेणाभिनिष्पद्यत एष आत्मेति होवाचैतदमृतमभयमेतद्ब्रह्मेति तस्य ह वा एतस्य ब्रह्मणो नाम सत्यमिति ॥

छान्दोग्योपनिषत्.

† द्रष्टृदर्शनदृश्यादिभावशून्यैकवस्तुनि ।
निर्विकारे निराकारे निर्विशेषे भिदा कुतः ॥
कल्पार्णव इवात्यन्तपरिपूर्णैकवस्तुनि ।
निर्विकारे निराकारे निर्विशेषे भिदाकुतः ॥
तेजसीवतमो यत्र प्रलीनं भ्रान्तिकारणम् ।
अद्वितीये परे तत्त्वे निर्विशेषे भिदा कुतः ॥

विवेकचूडामणिः

LXXVI—LXXVII.

THAT is the form of the highest Self wherein the world of subject and object though existing does not exist, and which though all *âkâśa* has no touch with it. It is all void and yet as if it were no void, the world is naught in it, it continues to be completely void though full of numberless worlds upon worlds.*

Yogavâsishtha.

LXXVIII.

THE whole of this cosmos is one self, there is no room for the idea of body and its like. Brahman is all that is, all bliss, whatever thou seest is all thought.†

Yogavâsishtha.

LXXIX.

AS light belongs to the sun, coldness to water, and heat to fire, so do existence, consciousness, bliss, eternity, immutable purity, belong, by nature, to self.‡

Âtmabodha.

---

* द्रष्टृदृश्यक्रमो यत्र स्थितोऽप्यस्तमयं गतः ।
यदनाकाशमाकाशं तद्रूपं परमात्मनः ॥
अशून्यमिव यच्छून्यं यस्मिन् शून्यं जगत्स्थितम् ।
सर्गौघे सति यच्छून्यं तद्रूपं परमात्मनः ॥

योगवासिष्ठम्.

† आत्मैवेदं जगत्सर्वं कुतोदेहादिकल्पना ।
ब्रह्मैवानन्दरूपं सद्यत्पश्यसि तदेव चित् ॥

योगवासिष्ठम्.

‡ प्रकाशोऽर्कस्य तोयस्य शैत्यमग्नेर्यथोष्णता ॥
स्वभावः सच्चिदानंदनित्यनिर्मलतात्मनः ॥

आत्मबोधः

LXXX.—LXXXI.

THE material cause of this illusion is none other than *Brahman*, the whole of the universe is, therefore, *Brahman*, and nothing else. *Brahman* being the All, causality is mere illusion ;—the real Truth being thus known there can be no room for the slightest separateness.*

Aparokshânubhuti.

LXXXII.

THIS Self is the bridge, the support, of the whole universe which, but for it, will be nowhere.†

Chândogyopanishad.

LXXXIII.

HE is all bliss of every kind, attaining this bliss it realizes its nature which is all bliss.‡

Taittiriyopanishad.

LXXXIV.

* * THIS therefore is the last measure of all bliss.§

Taittiriyopanishad.

---

* उपादानं प्रपञ्चस्य ब्रह्मणोन्यन्न विद्यते ।
तस्मात्सर्वप्रपञ्चोऽयं ब्रह्मैवास्ति न चेतरत् ॥
व्याप्यव्यापकता मिथ्या सर्वमात्मेतिशासनात् ।
इति ज्ञाते परे तत्त्वे भेदस्यावसरः कुतः ॥

अपरोक्षानुभूतिः

† अथ य आत्मा स सेतुर्विधृतिरेषां लोकानामसम्भेदाय ॥

छान्दोग्योपनिषत्.

‡ रसो वै सः । रसंह्येवायं लब्ध्वानन्दी भवति ॥

तैत्तिरीयोपनिषत्.

§ * * सैषानन्दस्य मीमांसा भवति

तैत्तिरीयोपनिषत्.

LXXXV.

THE one ever-effulgent stands concealed in all beings, It pervades every knowable object and is the inner self of all. It is the witness of all action, the all-embracing resort of beings, the unaffected seer, all thought, unique, and without properties.*

S'vetâśvataropanishad.

LXXXVI.

HE has neither form nor instruments, He is not seen as equal to or greater than (any thing); His transcendent power is heard of as unimaginably multifarious, omniscience and omnipotence constitute His very nature.†

S'vetâśvataropanishad.

LXXXVII.

NEITHER sun nor moon nor fire enlightens it; that indeed is my sublime habitat; thence no return is ever possible.‡

Bhagavadgitâ.

---

* एको देवः सर्वभूतेषु गूढः
सर्वव्यापी सर्व भूतान्तरात्मा ।
कर्माऽध्यक्षः सर्वभूताधिवासः
साक्षी चेता केवलो निर्गुणश्च ॥

श्वेताश्वतरोपनिषत्.

† न तस्य कार्यं करणं च विद्यते ।
न तत्समश्चाभ्यधिकश्च दृश्यते ॥
परास्य शक्तिर्विविधैव श्रूयते ।
स्वाभाविकी ज्ञानबलक्रिया च ॥

श्वेताश्वतरोपनिषत्.

‡ न तद्भासयते सूर्यो न शशाङ्को न पावकः ॥
यद्गत्वा न निवर्तन्ते तद्धाम परमं मम ॥

भगवद्गीता.

LXXXVIII.

THE Lord creates neither the objects nor the subjects which make up the world; nor does He plan the relation of ends and means;—nature alone continues to act.*

Bhagvadgitâ.

LXXXIX.

IT is unborn, ever awake, free from dream, having no form or no name. It is one continuous thought, all-knowing. There is no metaphor whatever in saying this.†

Gaudapâddchârya.

XC.

THIS oh Satyakáma is *Brahman* higher as well as lower, (*i. e.* science and nescience all is *Brahman*).‡

Praśnopanishad.

XCI.—XCII.

AS above so below, as below so above; he passes from death to death who here finds the least shadow of variety. There is no variety in This, It should be grasped

---

* न कर्तृत्वं न कर्माणि लोकस्य सृजति प्रभुः ॥
न कर्मफलसंयोगं स्वभावस्तु प्रवर्तते ॥

भगवद्गीता.

† अजमनिद्रमस्वप्नमनामकमरूपकम् ।
सकृद्विभातं सर्वज्ञं नोपचारः कथञ्चन ॥

गौडपादाचार्याः

‡ एतद्वै सत्यकाम परञ्चापरञ्च ब्रह्म ॥

प्रश्नोपनिषत्.

by the mind alone; he, indeed, passes from death to death who here finds the least shadow of variety*

Kathopanishad.
also *Bṛhadâraṇyakopanishad.*

XCIII.

AS a hawk or an eagle having soared high in the air wings its way back to its resting-place, being so far fatigued, so does the soul (having experienced the phenomenal) return into itself where it can sleep beyond all desires, beyond all dreams.†

Bṛhadâraṇyakopanishad.

XCIV.

THE sun does not shine there nor the moon nor the stars nor even these lightnings, least of all this fire; everything becomes enlightened in its light, the whole of this shines through Its lustre.‡

Kathopanishad also *Muṇdakopanishad.*

---

* यदेवेहतदमुत्र यदमुत्रतदन्विह ।
मृत्योः स मृत्युमाप्नोति य इह नानेव पश्यति ॥
मनसैवेदमाप्तव्यन्नेह नानास्ति किञ्चन ॥
मृत्योः स मृत्युङ्गच्छति य इह नानेव पश्यति ॥

कठोपनिषत्. । बृहदारण्यकोपनिषत्.

† तद्यथाऽस्मिन्नाकाशे श्येनो वा सुपर्णो वा विपरिपत्य श्रान्तः संहत्य पक्षौ सल्लयायैव ध्रियत एवमेवाऽयं पुरुष एतस्मा अन्ताय धावति यत्र सुप्तो न कञ्चन कामं कामयते न कञ्चन स्वप्नं पश्यति ॥

बृहदारण्यकोपनिषत्.

‡ न तत्र सूर्यो भाति न चन्द्रतारकं
नेमा विद्युतो भान्ति कुतोऽयमग्निः ।
तमेव भान्तमनुभाति सर्वं
तस्यभासा सर्वमिदं विभाति ॥

कठोपनिषत्. । मुण्डकोपनिषत्.

III.—SELF—IDENTITY.

XCV.

A particle of Its bliss supplies the bliss of the whole universe, everything becomes enlightened in Its light; nay all else appears worthless after a sight of that essence;—I am indeed this supreme eternal *Brahman*.*

Vijnânanaukâ.

XCVI.

THE power of sun, moon, fire and even of speech having exhausted itself to rest, the senses being all put out, that which stands self-illumined, beyond all relations, sending forth this universe of ideas, and all thought, is shown in the *S'rutis* to be the inner self of all.†

Svârâjyasiddhi.

---

* यदानन्दलेशैः समानन्दि विश्वं
यदाभाति सत्त्वे तदाभाति सर्वम् ।
यदालोचने हेयमन्यत्समस्तं
परं ब्रह्म नित्यं तदेवाहमस्मि ॥

विज्ञाननौका.

† संशान्ते रविशशिवह्निवाक्प्रकाशे
निर्वाणे करणगणे निरस्तसङ्गः ।
स्वज्योतिः प्रकटितवासनामयार्थ-
श्चिद्धातुः श्रुतिभिरुदीरितोऽन्तरात्मा ॥

स्वाराज्यसिद्धिः

XCVII.

I am without character, without action, without imagination, without relation, without change, without form, without sin, all eternity, ever liberated.*

Átmabodha.

XCVIII.

If thou objectest 'how I should grasp this?' Pray do not grasp it, ; for the *residuum* after all grasping is at end, is none other than thy-self.†

Panchadaśi.

XCIX.

WHERE is the man who doubts the fact of his own existence? for if such a one be found he should be told that the one who thus doubts is the Self he denies.‡

Svâtmanirupaṇa.

---

* निर्गुणो निष्क्रियो नित्यो निर्विकल्पो निरंजनः ।
निर्विकारो निराकारो नित्यमुक्तोऽस्मि निर्मलः ॥

आत्मबोधः

† कथं तादृङ्मयाग्राह्य इति चेन्मैव गृह्यताम् ।
सर्वग्रहोपसंशान्तौ स्वयमेवावशिष्यते ॥

पञ्चदशी.

‡ अस्ति स्वयमित्यस्मिन्नर्थे कस्याऽस्ति संशयः पुंसः ।
तत्रापि संशयश्चेत्संशयिता यः स एव भवसि त्वम् ॥

स्वात्मनिरूपणम्.

C.

NO other knowledge is necessary in *knowing* ones self, for the self is all knowledge ;—the lamp requires not the light of another lamp for its own illumination.*

Átmabodha.

CI.

SETTING aside every thing which becomes the object of knowledge in this world, there yet remains a residuum, the real essence of knowledge. The knowledge that this is *Brahman* is true knowledge of *Brahman.*†

Panchadaśi.

CII.

IT is the ear of ears, the mind of minds, the speech of speech, the breath of breaths, the eye of eyes. The wise transcending these (*i. e.* the physical ear, mind etc.) and renouncing this world of experience, rest in eternal immortality.‡

Kenopanishad.

CIII—CIV.

THIS Self in my heart is smaller than a grain of rice or barley or mustard, smaller than a grain of the *Syámáka* or even than a part of its part. This Self in my heart is bigger

---

* स्वबोधे नान्यबोधेच्छा बोधरूपतयात्मनः ॥
न दीपस्यान्यदीपेच्छा यथा स्वात्मप्रकाशने ॥

आत्मबोधः

† यस्मिन्यस्मिन्नस्ति लोके बोधस्तत्तदुपेक्षणे ।
यद्बोधमात्रं तद्ब्रह्मेत्येवं धीर्ब्रह्मनिश्चयः ॥

पञ्चदशी.

‡ श्रोत्रस्य श्रोत्रं मनसो मनो यद्वाचो ह वाचं स उ प्राणस्य प्राणश्चक्षुषश्चक्षुरतिमुच्य धीराः प्रेत्यास्माल्लोकादमृता भवन्ति ॥

केनोपनिषत्.

than the earth, more extensive than the atmosphere, wider than the sky, greater than all these worlds together. It is all action, all desire, all smell, all taste; It pervades all that is; It is void of speech (and all other senses), ever indifferent (to good or evil). This indeed is the Self in my heart, this indeed is *Brahman*. He becomes this *Brahman*, after passing away from here, who has faith in the Self, and has no doubt whatever.*

Chhândogyopanishad.

CV.

ALL this is *Brahman*, this Self is *Brahman*.†

Mâṇḍukyopanishad.

CVI.

AS the fool with eyes all bedimmed, sees the sun all dark, though covered only with a cloud, so does It appear in bondage only to the victims of illusion. I am this pure Self whose form is all eternal consciousness.‡

Hastâmalakastotra.

---

* एष म आत्माऽन्तर्हृदयेऽणीयान् व्रीहेर्वा यवाद्वा सर्षपाद्वा श्यामाकाद्वा श्यामाकतण्डुलाद्वा एष म आत्मान्तर्हृदये ज्यायान् पृथिव्या ज्यायानन्तरिक्षाज्ज्याया-न्दिवो ज्यायानेभ्यो लोकेभ्यः ॥

सर्वकर्मा सर्वकामः सर्वगन्धः सर्वरसः सर्वमिदमभ्यात्तोऽवाक्यनादर एष म आत्मान्तर्हृदय एतद्ब्रह्मैतमितः प्रेत्याभिसम्भविताऽस्मीति यस्य स्यादद्धान विचि-कित्सास्ति ॥

छान्दोग्योपनिषत्.

† सर्वं ह्येतद् ब्रह्मायमात्मा ब्रह्म ॥

माण्डुक्योपनिषत्.

‡ घनच्छन्नदृष्टिर्घनच्छन्नमर्कं
यथा मन्यते निष्प्रभं चातिमूढः ।
तथा बद्धवद्भाति यो मूढदृष्टेः
स नित्योपलब्धिस्वरूपोऽहमात्मा ॥

हस्तामलकस्तोत्रम्.

CVII.

IT is the one pervading all, but ever untouched by any, and therefore ever pure, and all clear, like (the all-pervading) *Âkâśa*. I am this pure Self whose form is all eternal consciousness.*

Hastâmalakastotra.

CVIII.

IT is without mind, without eyes, without any similar means (of relating itself to the objective), but all the same, it is the mind as well as the eye of all minds and all eyes, nay the means of means ;—Its form being ever incomprehensible by the mind, the eyes, and the rest. I am this pure Self, all eternal consciousness.†

Hastâmalakastotra.

CIX.

I am indeed that Supreme eternal *Brahman* which is all bliss, all light, beyond illusion, beyond conditions, realiz-

---

* समस्तेषु वस्तुष्वनुस्यूतमेकं
समस्तानि वस्तूनि यन्न स्पृशन्ति ।
वियद्वत्सदा शुद्धमच्छस्वरूपं
स नित्योपलब्धिस्वरूपोऽहमात्मा ॥

हस्तामलकस्तोत्रम्.

† मनश्चक्षुरादेर्वियुक्तः स्वयं यो
मनश्चक्षुरादेर्मनश्चक्षुरादिः ।
मनश्चक्षुरादेरगम्यस्वरूपः
स नित्योपलब्धिस्वरूपोऽहमात्मा ॥

हस्तामलकस्तोत्रम्

able only in the idea 'I am *Brahman*' the ever transcendent* Fourth.†

Vijnânanaukâ.

CX.

IT is this infinite atom, all this is that Self from end to end, It is the Truth, It is the Self;—oh S'vetaketu! THOU ART THAT.‡

Chhândogyopanishad.

CXI.

AS a lump of salt melted in water cannot be experienced by the eye, but only by the tongue, so indeed the ever-existent *Brahman* shining in the depth of the heart cannot be realized by the (external) senses, but by the light of that sympathetic awakening which comes from the word of a teacher. THOU indeed ART this *BRAHMAN*, not the phenomenal that appears around.§

Svârâjyasiddhi.

---

* That is to say *Vis'hva, Taijasa, Prâjna* are the three transcending which is the Fourth, *Brahman.*

† यदानंदरूपं प्रकाशस्वरूपं
निरस्तप्रपञ्चं परिच्छेदशून्यम् ।
अहंब्रह्मवृत्त्यैकगम्यं तुरीयं
परं ब्रह्म नित्यं तदेवाहमस्मि ॥

विज्ञाननौका.

‡ स य एषोऽणिमैतदात्म्यमिदं सर्वं तत्सत्यं स आत्मा तत्त्वमसि श्वेतकेतो ॥

छान्दोग्योपनिषद्.

§ अप्सु प्रलीनमिव सैन्धवखिल्यमक्ष्णा
पश्यन्ति यन्न करणैरपि हृद्विभातम् ।
विन्दन्ति यद्रसनयेव रसं गुरूक्त्या
तद्ब्रह्म तत्त्वमसि दृश्यमिदं तु न त्वम् ॥

स्वाराज्यसिद्धिः

CXII.

THE ocean transformed, through the action of clouds, into the form of rivers etc., ceases to be itself; so indeed hast thou forgotten thyself through the power of conditions. Oh friend! remember thy full Self, THOU ART *BRAHMAN*, the ground of existence, the All.*

Svârâjyasiddhi.

CXIII.

WHERE there is anything like duality there alone does one see another, there alone does one smell another, there alone does one hear another, there alone does one speak to another, there alone does one think of another, there alone does one know another. But when all is one Self to him, what should he smell with what? what should he see with what? what should he hear with what? what should he speak of with what? what should he think of with what? what should he know with what? By what indeed should that be known through which everything proceeds to know? By what should the Knower be known?†

Bṛhadâraṇyakopanishad.

---

* अब्धिर्यथा जलधरैरपनीयनीतो
नद्यादिभावमुदधित्वमति जहौ स्वाम् ।
एवं भवानुपधिभिः खलु विस्मृतः स्वं
सद्ब्रह्म तत्त्वमसि संस्मर पूर्णभावम् ॥

स्वाराज्यसिद्धिः

† यत्र हि द्वैतमिव भवति तदितर इतरं पश्यति तदितर इतरं जिघ्रति तदितर इतरं शृणोति तदितर इतरमभिवदति तदितर इतरं मनुते तदितर इतरं विजानाति यत्र वा अस्य सर्वमात्मात्मैवाऽभूत्तत्केन कं जिघ्रेत्तत्केन कं पश्येत्तत्केन कं शृणुयात्तत्केन कमभिवदेत्तत्केन कं मन्वीत तत्केन कं विजानीयाद्येनेदं सर्वं विजानाति तं केन विजानीयाद्विज्ञातारमरे केन विजानीयात् ॥

बृहदारण्यकोपनिषत्.

CXIV.

IT is not attainable by the most constant attendance at lectures, many though hearing numerous such never know what It is. Strange indeed is the speaker who speaks of It, stranger still who obtains It, but most strange of all is he who, being properly instructed by a competent (teacher) realizes It (in himself and all).*

Kathopanishad.

CXV.

ONE rare soul sees It like something strange, another speaks of It in the same strain as of something extraordinary, a third hears It as something uncommon, while a fourth though constantly hearing knows It not in the least.†

Bhagvadgitâ.

IV.—THE MEANS.

CXVI.—CXVII.

TILL study should not allay in thee the sense of separateness, the mind cannot take on the form of that (essence) and thou canst not realize *Brahman*. Four indeed, are

---

* श्रवणायाऽपि बहुभिर्यो न लभ्यः
शृण्वन्तोऽपि बहवो यन्न विद्युः ।
आश्चर्यो वक्ता कुशलोऽस्य लब्धा-
श्चर्यो ज्ञाता कुशलानुशिष्टः ॥

कठोपनिषत्.

† आश्चर्यवत्पश्यति कश्चिदेन-
माश्चर्यवद्वदति तथैव चान्यः ।
आश्चर्यवच्चैनमन्यः शृणोति
श्रुत्वाप्येनं वेद न चैव कश्चित् ॥

भगवद्गीता.

the gatekeepers at the entrance of the palace of liberation :—

(1) Self-restraint, (2) Contemplation, (3) Contentment, (4) Company of the wise.*

Yogavâsishtha.

CXVIII.

HE alone escapes from the web of illusion, this world, even like the lord of beasts from the trap which holds him fast, who, with all acts, all pleasures, attuned to the supreme aim, puts forth strong personal effort in that behalf.†

Yogavâsishtha.

CXIX.—CXX.

TREES continue to vegetate, and so do live on beasts and birds; he alone *lives* whose mind lives *not* in consequence of taking on a variety of forms. All holy writ is so much burden to him who has no discrimination, all philosophy is so much burden to him whose germ of desire is not destroyed ; the

---

* यावदभ्यासयोगेन न शान्ता भेदधीस्तव ।
नूनं तावदतद्रूपो न ब्रह्म परिपश्यसि ॥
मोक्षद्वारे द्वारपालाश्चत्वारः परिकीर्तिताः ।
शमो विचारः सन्तोषश्चतुर्थः साधुसङ्गमः ॥

योगवासिष्ठम्.

† यस्तूदारचमत्कारः सदाचारविहारवान् ।
स निर्याति जगन्मोहान्मृगेन्द्रः पञ्जरादिव ॥

योगवासिष्ठम्.

mind is so much burden to him who has not acquired self-control, the body is so much burden to him who knows only the *anâtman* (non-self.)*

Yogavâsishtha.

CXXI.

THERE can be no man more despicable than him who does not put into practice the words of the trustworthy proficient who explains, with great pains, (the real truth), on being questioned.†

Yogavâsishtha.

CXXII.—CXXIII.

ALL desire is ignorance, the destruction of desire is liberation, and this liberation oh Râma ! is easily brought about only by ceasing to desire. The mind experiences bondage from the firm conviction 'I am not *Brahman*,' it realizes entire freedom, from the equally firm conviction 'I am *Brahman*.'‡

Yogavâsishtha.

---

* तरवोऽपि हि जीवन्ति जीवन्ति मृगपक्षिणः ।
स जीवति मनो यस्य मननेन न जीवति ॥
भारोऽविवेकिनः शास्त्रं भारो ज्ञानं च रागिणः ।
अशान्तस्य मनो भारो भारोऽनात्मविदो वपुः ॥

योगवासिष्ठम्.

† प्रामाणिकस्य तज्ज्ञस्य वक्तुः पृष्टस्य यत्नतः ।
नानुतिष्ठति यो वाक्यं नान्यस्तस्मान्नराधमः ॥

योगवासिष्ठम्.

‡ इच्छामात्रमविद्येह तन्नाशो मोक्ष उच्यते ।
सचासङ्कल्पमात्रेण सिद्धो भवति राघव ॥
नाहं ब्रह्मेतिसङ्कल्पात्सुदृढाद्बध्यते मनः ।
अहं ब्रह्मेति सङ्कल्पात्सुदृढान्मुच्यते मनः ॥

योगवासिष्ठम्.

CXXIV.

HE continually sees the Self who studies to unify philosophy, and the teacher's explanations, with the facts of his own consciousness.*

Yogavâsishtha.

CXXV.

THE light breaking in upon the mind should not be kept off by having recourse to that false logic which puts forth unholy guesses of every kind up to the obliteration even of the facts of consciousness.†

Yogavâsishtha.

CXXVI.—CXXVII.

With no confidence in the facts of his own consciousness, and with the obvious endlessness of argumentation, how would he who poses himself as a Professor of Logic, obtain conviction of Truth? If argumentation is meant as a help to the intellect, you are welcome to argue in accord with

---

* स्वानुभूतेश्च शास्त्रस्य गुरोश्चैवैकवाक्यता ।
यस्याभ्यासेन तेनात्मा संततेनावलोक्यते ॥

योगवासिष्ठम्.

† न कुतार्किकतामेत्य नाशनीया प्रबुद्धता ।
अनुभूत्यपलापान्तैरपवित्रैः कुकल्पनैः ॥

योगवासिष्ठम्.

the facts of your consciousness, but certainly not to argue without aim, in any line you choose.*

Panchadas'i.

CXXVIII.

THE sense of this can never be gathered by ratiocination alone, oh beloved one! it leads to real knowledge only when used by one who really knows. This knowing is that which thou, oh child of truth! hast already acquired;—oh Nachiketas! there indeed can be no better questioner than thyself.†

Kathopanishad.

CXXIX—CXXXI.

THIS self is not realizable by study, nay not even by intelligence or much learning. The Self unfolds its full essence to him alone who applies his self to self. He who has not given up the ways of vice, he who is not able to control himself, he who is not at peace within,

---

* स्वानुभूतावविश्वासे तर्कस्याप्यनवस्थितेः ।
कथं वा तार्किकंमन्यस्तत्त्वनिश्चयमाप्नुयात् ।
बुध्यारोहाय तर्कश्चेदपेक्षेत तथा सति ।
स्वानुभूत्यनुसारेण तर्क्यतां मा कुतर्क्यताम् ॥

पञ्चदशी.

† नैषा तर्केण मतिरापनेया
प्रोक्तान्येनैव सुज्ञानाय प्रेष्ठ ।
यान्त्वमापः सत्यधृतिर्बतासि
त्वादृङ्नो भूयान्नचिकेतः प्रष्टा ॥

कठोपनिषद्

he whose mind is not at rest, can never realize the self, though full of all the learning in the world. That which lies at the root of all distinctions of caste and creed is its food, even death itself is its drink ;—who (not so prepared) can know what It is ? *

Kathopanishad.

CXXXII.

HOW can books enlighten that lump of clay fashioned in the form of man, who does not in any manner realize the Truth explained to him with all possible clearness.†

Naishkarmyasiddhi.

---

* नायमात्मा प्रवचनेन लभ्यो
न मेधया न बहुना श्रुतेन ।
यमेवैष वृणुते तेन लभ्य-
स्तस्यैष आत्मा विवृणुते तनूं स्वाम् ॥

कठोपनिषत् । मुण्डकोपनिषत्.

नाविरतो दुश्चरितान्नाशान्तो नासमाहितः ।
नाशान्तमानसो वापि प्रज्ञानेनैनमाप्नुयात् ॥
यस्य ब्रह्म च क्षत्रञ्च उभे भवत ओदनम्
मृत्युर्यस्योपसेचनं क इत्था वेद यत्र सः ॥

कठोपनिषत्.

† बोधेऽप्यनुभवो यस्य न कथञ्चन जायते ।
तं कथं बोधयेच्छास्त्रं लोष्टं नरसमाकृतिम् ॥

नैष्कर्म्यसिद्धिः

CXXXIII.

WE rejoice with those whom we recognise as centred in self-realization ; the rest we pity ; with the deluded we do not care to argue.*

Panchadaśi.

CXXXIV.

TALK as much philosophy as you please, worship as many gods as you like, observe all ceremonies, sing devoted praises of any number of deities ;—liberation never comes, even at the end of a hundred *kalpas*, without realization of the oneness of self.†

Vivekachudamaṇi.

CXXXV.

WHO knows *Vidyâ* and *Avidyâ* together, passes beyond death through *avidyâ*, and enters immortality through *Vidyâ.*‡

Iśopanishad.

---

* ज्ञात्वा सदा तत्त्वनिष्ठाननुमोदामहे वयम् ।
अनुशोचाम एवान्यान्भ्रान्तैर्विवदामहे ॥

पञ्चदशी.

† वदन्तु शास्त्राणि यजन्तु देवा-
न्कुर्वन्तु कर्माणि भजन्तु देवताः ।
आत्मैक्यबोधेन विनापि मुक्ति-
र्न सिद्ध्यति ब्रह्मशतान्तरेऽपि ॥

विवेकचूडामणिः.

‡ विद्याञ्चाविद्याञ्च यस्तद्वेदोभयं सह ।
अविद्यया मृत्युं तीर्त्वा विद्ययाऽमृतमश्नुते ॥

ईशोपनिषत्.

CXXXVI.

THE good is one thing, the agreeable another; men find them in a variety of objects and become bound, one way or other. He who attaches himself to the (supreme) good reaps the highest bliss, he who persues the agreeable is cheated of the real object (of existence).*

Kathopanishad.

CXXXVII—CXXXVIII.

THESE (*i.e.* the good and the agreeable), thou knowest, are *Vidyâ* and *Avidyâ*, opposed one to the other in their very nature, and having entirely different results in store. Oh Nachiketas ! the various desires I propose to thee fail to move, thou art really devoted to *vidyâ* alone. Groping about in (the night of) *Avidyâ*, fools flatter themselves with wisdom and learning, and continue to tumble about, without end, like the blind led by the blind.†

Kathopanishad ; *Muṇdakopanishad.*

CXXXIX—CXLI.

THE lyre with all the beauty of its make, and the melody of its music, serves at best to please the hearer, it cannot lead to universal empire. In the same manner all the flow of speech, all the stream of sweet words, all the skill expended

---

* अन्यच्छ्रेयोऽन्यदुतैव प्रेयस्ते उभे नानार्थे पुरुषं सिनीतः । तयोः श्रेय आददानस्य साधु भवति हीयतेऽर्थाद्य उ प्रेयो वृणीते ॥

कठोपनिषत्.

† दूरमेते विपरीते विषूची अविद्या या च विद्येति ज्ञाता ।
विद्याऽभीप्सिनन्नचिकेतसं मन्ये न त्वा कामा बहवो लोलुपन्ते ॥
अविद्यायामन्तरे वर्तमानाः स्वयन्धीराः पण्डितम्मन्यमानाः ।
दन्द्रम्यमाणा परियन्ति मूढा अन्धेनैव नीयमाना यथाऽन्धाः ॥

कठोपनिषत् । मुण्डकोपनिषत्.

on explaining philosophy,—all that the learned call learning, has the belly, not the self, for its end. Vain is the study of philosophy if it leads not to the Essence, equally vain is all philosophy if the Essence is realized.*

Vivekachudâmaṇi.

CXLII.—CXLIII.

DISEASE disappears not with the mere name of medicine, but by actually swallowing it ; talking of *Brahman*, without proper realization, can never bring about liberation. Till the objective is not dissolved (in the subject), till the essence of self is not realized, no liberation can come from speaking about *Brahman*,—all the fruit of such activity is only (waste of) so much breath.†

Vivekachudâmaṇi.

---

* वीणाया रूपसौन्दर्य्यं तन्त्रीवादनसौष्ठवम् ।
प्रजारञ्जनमात्रं तन्न साम्राज्याय कल्पते ॥
वाग्वैखरी शब्दझरी शास्त्रव्याख्यानकौशलम् ।
वैदुष्यं विदुषां तद्वद्भुक्तये न तु मुक्तये ॥
अविज्ञाते परे तत्त्वे शास्त्राधीतिस्तु निष्फला ।
विज्ञातेऽपि परे तत्त्वे शास्त्राधीतिस्तु निष्फला ॥

विवेकचूडामणिः

† न गच्छति विना पानं व्याधिरौषधशब्दतः ।
विना परोक्षानुभवं ब्रह्मशब्दैर्न मुच्यते ॥
अकृत्वा दृश्यविलयमज्ञात्वा तत्त्वमात्मनः ।
ब्रह्मशब्दैः कुतो मुक्तिरुक्तिमात्रफलैर्नृणाम् ॥

विवेकचूडामणिः

iii.—The Aspirant.

CXLIV—CXLV.

THE knowing intellect skilled in grasping the *pros* and *cons* of every theme, and cleared of all dross by the means just described, is the true aspirant after self-knowledge. Discrimination, non-attachment, self-control and its accompaniments, keen desire of liberation, these make one fit to inquire after *Brahman.**

Vivekachudâmaṇi.

CXLVI—CXLVIII.

THIS Self cannot be realized by want of (spiritual) strength, by indifference, by austerities unaccompanied with renunciation. The self of that knower who applies himself to self with the means described enters the great Self—*Brahman*. Sages having found It, stand ever content in *gnosis*, remain centred in the Self, being free from all attachment, and always at peace within and without. They find the unconditioned and all-pervading, and realizing It within, become one with the All. With faith firmly fixed in the teaching of the *Vedânta*, with the mind entirely purified through renunciation and *gnosis*, ascetics, one with the immortal, become liberated in

---

* मेधावी पुरुषो विद्वानूहापोहविचक्षणः।
अधिकार्य्यात्मविद्यायामुक्तलक्षणलक्षितः॥
विवेकिनो विरक्तस्य शमादिगुणशालिनः।
मुमुक्षोरेव हि ब्रह्मजिज्ञासायोग्यता मता॥

विवेकचूडामणिः

Brahman (*i.e.* become one with Brahman) at the moment of dissolution.*

Mundakopanishad.

CXLIX.

IN the air or in water no mark is seen of the passage of birds or fishes; so is entirely inscrutable the passage of the knowers (of *Brahman*).†

Sánkaráchárya.

CL.

THE eye perceives not sound, being dissimilar by nature; the material eye cannot see the (spiritual) self.‡

Naishkarmyasiddhi.

---

*नायमात्मा बलहीनेन लभ्यो न च प्रमादात्तपसो वाप्यलिङ्गात् ।
एतैरुपायैर्यतते यस्तु विद्वांस्तस्यैष आत्मा विशते ब्रह्मधाम ॥
संप्राप्यैनमृषयो ज्ञानतृप्ताः
कृतात्मानो वीतरागाः प्रशान्ताः ।
ते सर्वगं सर्वतः प्राप्य धीरा
युक्तात्मानः सर्वमेवाविशन्ति ॥
वेदान्तविज्ञानसुनिश्चितार्थाः
सन्यासयोगाद्यतयः शुद्धसत्त्वाः ।
ते ब्रह्मलोकेषु परान्तकाले
परामृताः परिमुच्यन्ति सर्वे ॥

मुण्डकोपनिषत्.

† शकुनीनामिवाकाशे जले वारिचरस्य च ।
पदं यथा न दृश्येत तथा ज्ञानविदां गतिः ॥

शङ्कराचार्याः

‡ चक्षुर्न वीक्षते शब्दमतदात्मत्वकारणात् ।
यथैवं भौतिकी दृष्टिर्नात्मानं परिपश्यति ॥

नैष्कर्म्यसिद्धिः

CLI.

AS the face is fully reflected in a clear glass, so in the body of the true seeker the *Âtman* is reflected in the intellect.*

Âtmapurâṇa.

CLII.

THE *Ṛk* says: this *Brahmavidyâ* should be given to those alone who observe all ceremonies, who have learnt and do respect the *Veda*, who have faith in *Brahman*, who keep the *Ekarṡi*-fire, who are full of faith, and who have duly passed through the *S'irovrata.*†

Muṇdakopanishad.

CLIII.

HE *knows* who finds a teacher; he (then) delays only so long as he is not free (from the body), for on being so free he is one with the All.‡

Chhândogyopanishad.

---

* यथा विशुद्ध आदर्शे विस्पष्टं दृश्यते मुखम् ।
अधिकारिशरीरेस्मिन्बुद्धावात्मा तथैव हि ॥

आत्मपुराणम्.

† तदेतदृचाभ्युक्तं क्रियावन्तः श्रोत्रिया ब्रह्मनिष्ठाः ।
स्वयं जुह्वते एकर्षिं श्रद्धयन्तस्तेषामेवैतां ब्रह्मविद्यां
वदेत शिरोव्रतं विधिवद्यैस्तु चीर्णम् ॥

मुण्डकोपनिषत्.

‡ आचार्यवान्पुरुषो वेद तस्य तावदेव चिरं यावन्न विमोक्ष्येऽथ सम्पत्स्य इति ॥

छान्दोग्योपनिषत्.

CLIV.

HAVING obtained this priceles birth with all the senses in their full activity, he who does not understand the good of self, destroys himself.*

Mahâ-Bhârata,

CLV.

THE boat—this body—has been chartered by thee at the heaviest price—all thy good acts,—to cross over to the other side of this ocean of sin and sorrow. Pray pass on while it does not break.†

Miscellaneous.

CLVI.

THOSE who destroy (their) Self, go, after death, to the sphere called *Asurya* (without the sun), all enveloped in thick darkness.‡

Isopanishad; Bṛhadâraṇyakopanishad.

---

* प्राप्य चानुत्तमं जन्म लब्ध्वा चेन्द्रियसौष्ठवम् ।
न वेत्त्यात्महितं यस्तु स भवेदात्मघातकः ॥

महाभारतम्.

† महता पुण्यपण्येन क्रीतेयं कायनौस्त्वया ।
पारं दुःखोदधेर्गन्तुं तर यावन्न भिद्यते ॥

प्रास्ताविकः

‡ असूर्या नाम ते लोका अन्धेन तमसा वृताः ।
तांस्ते प्रेत्याभिगच्छन्ति ये के चात्महनो जनाः ॥

ईशोपनिषत्। बृहदारण्यकोपनिषत्.

CLVII.

THE ignorant, the faithless, and the sceptic, meets with destruction; neither this world nor the next (belongs to him);—he who is all doubt can find no happiness whatever.*

Bhagavadgitâ.

---

iv.—The teacher.

CLVIII—CLIX.

TILL thy mind reaches the stage of (intuitive) development, follow what is assured thee by teachers, books and the (logical) instruments of knowledge. When thus is burnt out all latent desire and the Thing is realized, thou shouldst not hesitate to give up all concern even with these, however good or useful they be.†

Yogavâshitha.

CLX—CLXI.

BY books (*Sâstra*) is meant all that is offered by way of explaining the facts of nature, by great souls free from likes and dislikes, with eyes trained to observation and

---

* अज्ञश्चाश्रद्दधानश्च संशयात्मा विनश्यति ॥
नायं लोकोऽस्ति न परो न सुखं संशयात्मनः ॥

भगवद्गीता.

† अव्युत्पन्नमना यावद्भवानज्ञाततत्पदः ।
गुरुशास्त्रप्रमाणैस्तु निर्णीतं तावदाचर ॥
ततः पक्वकषायेण नूनं विज्ञातवस्तुना ।
शुभोऽप्यसौ त्वया त्याज्यो वासनौघो निरोधिना ॥

योगवासिष्ठम्.

reason. Those resolute souls who are full of the highest goodness, who are equal to all, and who are possessed of a tact peculiar to themselves, are the really wise.*

Yogavâsishtha.

CLXII.

I (thus informed) am yet only versed in the (words of the) *Mantras* (the sacred hymns), I know nothing of Self. I have heard from sages of your stamp that the knower of Self rises above all sorrow. (With all my learning) I am full of discontent and sorrow, oh Lord! take me to the other side of this ocean of misery.†

Chhândogyopanishad.

CLXIII.

THIS *Brahman* should be explained by the father to his eldest son, or (by the teacher) to a properly (sympathetic) pupil, and to no one else.‡

Chhândogyopanishad.

---

* अविसंवादिनार्थे यद्यत्प्रामाणिकदृष्टिभिः ।
वीतरागैर्विनिर्णीतं तच्छास्त्रमिति कथ्यते ॥
महासत्त्वगुणोपेता ये धीराः समदृष्टयः ।
अनिर्देश्यकलोपेताः साधवस्त उदाहृताः ॥

योगवासिष्ठम्.

† सोऽहं भगवो मन्त्रविदेवास्मि नात्मविच्छ्रुतं ह्येव मे भगवद्दृशेभ्यस्तरति शोकमात्मविदिति सोऽहं भगवः शोचामि तं मा भगवाञ्छोकस्य पारं तारयतु ।

छान्दोग्योपनिषत्.

‡ इदं वाव तज्ज्येष्ठाय पुत्राय पिता ब्रह्म प्रब्रूयात् प्राणाय्याय वान्तेवासिने नान्यस्मै कस्मै ।

छान्दोग्योपनिषत्.

CLXIV.

OH Râma ! the cause of (Self-)realization is none other than the pupil's own intelligence.*

Yogavâsishtha.

CLXV.

SELF should be raised, not destroyed, by Self ; for, Self alone is the friend and foe of Self.†

Bhagvadgitâ.

CLXVI—CLXVII.

ONE (course) leads to success in one birth or many, by gradual practice after the manner pointed out by the teacher; the other leads soon to real *gnosis* through the Self, aided even by moderate intellectual development, even like the fall of the fruit from above.‡

Yogavâsishtha.

---

* ज्ञप्तेस्तु कारणं राम शिष्यप्रज्ञैव केवलम् ॥

योगवासिष्ठम्.

† उद्धरेदात्मनात्मानं नात्मानमवसादयेत् ।
आत्मैव ह्यात्मनो बन्धुरात्मैव रिपुरात्मनः ॥

भगवद्गीता.

‡ एकस्तावद्गुरुप्रोक्तादनुष्ठानाच्छनैः शनैः ।
जन्मना जन्मभिर्वापि सिद्धिदः समुदाहृतः ॥
द्वितीयस्त्वात्मनैवाशु किंचिद्व्युत्पन्नचेतसा ।
भवति ज्ञानसम्प्राप्तिराकाशफलपातवत् ॥

योगवासिष्ठम्.

CLXVIII.

HAVING supported Self by Self, of one's own accord, through *thinking*, one should carry this deer—his own mind—across the ocean of delusion, this world.*

Yogavâsishtha.

CLXIX.

TELL me what thou seest as other than religion and non-religion, other than these effects or their causes, other than that which is past and that which is yet to come.†

Kathopanishad.

CLXX.

S'AUNAKA, the rich householder, approached Angirasa in due formality, and asked oh Lord! What is that whose knowledge leads to the knowledge of all that is? He replied: two sciences are taught by the knowers of *Brahman*, the Higher (*Vidyâ*) and the Lower (*Avidyâ*).‡

Muṇḍakopanishad.

---

* स्वयमेवात्मनात्मानमवष्टभ्य विचारतः ।
संसारमोहजलधेस्तारयेत्स्वमनोमृगम् ॥

योगवासिष्ठम्.

† अन्यत्र धर्मादन्यत्राधर्मा-
दन्यत्रास्मात्कृताकृतात् ।
अन्यत्र भूताच्च भव्याच्च
यत्तत्पश्यसि तद्वद ॥

कठोपनिषत्.

‡ शौनको ह वै महाशालोऽङ्गिरसं विधिवदुपसन्नः पप्रच्छ कस्मिन्नु भगवो विज्ञाते सर्वमिदं विज्ञातं भवतीति । तस्मै स होवाच । द्वे विद्ये वेदितव्ये इति ह स्म यद्ब्रह्मविदो वदन्ति परा चैवापरा च ॥

मुण्डकोपनिषत्.

CLXXI—CLXXIII.

THE ultimate aim of all *Veda*, the final result of all austerity, the object of keeping the period of studentship, I describe to thee in brief:—it is the syllable *Aum*. This is immutable *Brahman*, this is the highest Essence, it becomes whatever he desires to him who knows this, the ever-unchangeable. This, indeed, is the highest support, the greatest help, betaking himself to this he becomes glorified in *Brahman*.*

Kathopanishad.

CLXXIV.

THE knower of *Brahman* attains to the Supreme; hence is this (*ṛk*) said "*Brahman* is being, consciousness, limitlessness." He who realizes this, present in the heart (intellect) as well as in the highest *Âkâśa*, has access to the fruition of all desire whatever, at one sweep, being one with all-seeing *Brahman*.†

Taittiriyopanishad.

---

* सर्वे वेदा यत्पदमामनन्ति
तपांसि सर्वाणि च यद्वदन्ति ।
यदिच्छन्तो ब्रह्मचर्यञ्चरति
तत्ते पदं सङ्ग्रहेण ब्रवीम्योम् ॥
एतध्येवाक्षरं ब्रह्म एतदेवाक्षरम्परम् ।
एतदेवाक्षरं ज्ञात्वा यो यदिच्छति तस्य तत् ॥
एतदालम्बनं श्रेष्ठमेतदालम्बनं परम् ।
एतदालाम्बनं ज्ञात्वा ब्रह्मलोके महीयते ॥

कठोपनिषत्.

† ब्रह्मविदाप्नोति परम् । तदेषाभ्युक्ता । सत्यं ज्ञानमनन्तं ब्रह्म । यो वेद निहितं गुहायां परमे व्योमन् सोऽश्नुते सर्वान्कामान् सह ब्रह्मणा विपश्चितेति ॥

तैत्तिरीयोपनिषत्.

CLXXV.

THIS cosmos is all *Purusha*, all ceremonial, all austerities, the highest immortal *Brahman*. He who realizes this in the cavity of the heart, easily scatters into nothing, oh good one! the knot of *Avidyâ*, even in this life.*

Muṇdakopanishad.

CLXXVI.

THE wise knowing, through the practice of subjective concentration, the all-effulgent one, extremely difficult to see, concealed deep beyond everything, shining through all acts in every heart, inaccessible, and without beginning, transcends all pleasure and all pain.†

Kathopanishad.

CLXXVII.

HE who sees himself in all, and all in himself, attains to the empire of Self, thus worshipping Self and looking on all things with equal eye.‡

Manu.

---

* पुरुष एवेदं विश्वं कर्म तपो ब्रह्म परामृतम् । एतद्यो वेद निहितं गुहायां सोऽविद्याग्रन्थिं विकिरतीह सौम्य ॥

मुण्डकोपनिषत्.

† तन्दुर्दर्शंगूढमनुप्रविष्टं
गुहाहितं गव्हरेष्ठम्पुराणम् ।
अध्यात्मयोगाधिगमेन देवं
मत्वा धीरो हर्षशोकौ जहाति ॥

कठोपनिषत्.

‡ सर्वभूतेषु चात्मानं सर्वभूतानि चात्मनि ।
समं पश्यन्नात्मयाजी स्वाराज्यमधिगच्छति ॥

मनुः

CLXXVIII.

KNOWING the great all-pervading Self through whom is experienced the whole of dream and waking, the wise never become subject to sorrow.*

Kathopanishad.

CLXXIX—CLXXX.

AS surely as water showered on a table-land seeks the lower ground, so indeed does one seeing variety in the attributes (of *Brahman*), becomes attached to them (in future). As water poured upon a clear even surface stands ever pure and undefiled, so stands, oh Gautama! the Self of the silent *knower*.†

Kathopanishad.

CLXXXI.

THIS (body) is the city, with eleven gates,‡ of the ever unborn, all unfailing consciousness. He who knows this well never comes to grief, and is liberated twice§ over.‖

Kathopanishad.

---

* स्वप्नान्तं जागरितान्तं चोभौ येनानुपश्याति ।
महान्तं विभुमात्मानं मत्वा धीरो न शोचाति ॥

कठोपनिषत्.

† यथोदकन्दुर्गे वृष्टम्पर्वतेषु विधावाति ।
एवं धर्मान् पृथक् पश्यंस्तानेवानुविधावाति ॥
यथोदकं शुद्धे शुद्धमासिक्तन्तादृगेव भवति ।
एवम्मुनेर्विजानत आत्मा भवति गौतम ॥

कठोपनिषत्.

‡ The seven apertures in the head, the two apertures at the lower extremity of the trunk, the navel, and the crown of the head, make up the eleven gates.

§ That is to say, he is liberated by the act of self-realization even in this life, and stands no chance of re-birth even after death.

‖ पुरमेकादशद्वारमजस्यावक्रचेतसः ।
अनुष्ठाय न शोचाति विमुक्तश्च विमुच्यते ॥

कठोपनिषत्.

CLXXXII—CLXXXIII.

AS these rivers flowing to and gaining the ocean lose themselves in it, lose even their name and form, and become included in the name 'ocean,' so do all the sixteen forms of the objective flowing to and gaining the *purusha* become lost in him, lose even their name and form, and become included in the '*purusha*.' This (*purusha*) is the immortal transcending all forms of the objective. This is thus summed up:—That death may not overpower thee, know the only knowable, the *Purusha*, in whom are centred all forms like the radii of a chariot-wheel in its navel.*

Pras'nopanishad.

CLXXXIV.

KNOW that one Self alone with which are bound sky, earth, atmosphere, mind, and all the vital breaths;—leave aside all other speech;—this alone is the bridge (over the gulf of this world) to immortality.†

Muṇḍakopanishad.

---

* यथेमा नद्यः स्यन्दमानाः समुद्रायणाः समुद्रं प्राप्यास्तं गच्छन्ति भिद्येते तासां नामरूपे समुद्रइत्येवं प्रोच्यते । एवमेवास्य परिद्रष्टुरिमाः षोडशकलाः पुरुषायणाः पुरुषं प्राप्यास्तं गच्छन्ति भिद्येते तासां नामरूपे पुरुषइत्येवं प्रोच्यते स एषोऽकलोऽमृतो भवति तदेष श्लोकः

अराइव रथनाभौ कला यस्मिन्प्रतिष्ठिताः ।
तं वेद्यं पुरुषं वेद यथा मा वो मृत्युः परिव्यथाः ॥

प्रश्नोपनिषत्.

† यस्मिन् द्यौः पृथिवी चान्तरिक्षमोतं मनः सह प्राणैश्च सर्वैः ।
तमेवैकं जानथ आत्मानमन्या वाचो विमुञ्चथ अमृतस्यैष सेतुः ॥

मुण्डकोपनिषत्.

CLXXXV.

BRÂHMAṆAS disown him who knows other than self as a *Brâhmaṇa*, *Kshatriyas* disown him who knows other than self as a *Kshatriya*, the people disown him who knows other than self as the people, the gods disown him who knows other than self as a god, the spirits disown him who knows other than self as a spirit, everything disowns that which knows other than self as the thing,—all this "Self"—the *Brâhmaṇas*, the *Kshatriyas*, the people, the gods, the spirits, everything,—is *Brahman*.*

Bṛhadâraṇyakopanishad.

CLXXXVI.

THAT Self which is beyond decay, death, sorrow, which requires no food nor drink, which is all accomplished desire, all fulfilled thought, should be looked for, should be inquired after. He gains access to all worlds, has all his desires fulfilled, who, having known this Self, realizes It (fully in himself and all).†

Chhândogyopanishad.

---

* ब्रह्म तं परादाद्योऽन्यत्रात्मनो ब्रह्म वेद क्षत्रं तं परादाद्योऽन्यत्रात्मनः क्षत्रं वेद लोकास्तं परादुर्योऽन्यत्रात्मनो लोकान्वेद देवास्तं परादुर्योऽन्यत्रात्मनो देवान्वेद भूतानि तं परादुर्योऽन्यत्रात्मनो भूतानि वेद सर्वं तं परादाद्योऽन्यत्रात्मनः सर्वं वेदेदं ब्रह्मेदं क्षत्रमिमे लोका इमे देवा इमानि भूतानीदं सर्वं यदयमात्मा ॥

बृहदारण्यकोपनिषत्.

† य आत्मापहतपाप्मा विजरो विमृत्युर्विशोकोऽविजिघत्सोऽपिपासः सत्यकामः सत्यसङ्कल्पः सोऽन्वेष्टव्यः स विजिज्ञासितव्यः स सर्वांश्च लोकानाप्नोति सर्वांश्च कामान्यस्तमात्मानमनुविद्य विजानातीति ॥

छान्दोग्योपनिषत्.

CLXXXVII.

SAID Yâjnavalkya to the Emperor (Janaka):—The same has been explained by the *Ṛk* as well: this, indeed, is the eternal glory of him who has realized *Brahman*. It neither grows nor is diminished by doing or not doing any act, the knower *knows* this very truth. Knowing this, he is not affected by any *Karma* whatever, all being as sin to him. The heat of his senses cools down into that calmness of mind which follows on absence of desire, all kind of latent attachment leaves him, no conditions disturb him, ecstatic trance environs him,—who knowing thus sees Self in Self, sees the All as Self. No good or evil touches him, he transcends all good and all evil. The fulfilment or non-fulfilment of any (secular or temporal) act affects him not, he having reduced them all to nothing. He is beyond all form, beyond all desire, beyond all doubt. This is the real *Brâhmaṇa*, this is the real condition of *Brahman*.*

Bṛhadâraṇyakopanishad.

CLXXXVIII.

ONE'S own sphere (of life) though inferior is preferable to that of another even if it were superior. Death in one's own sphere is most desirable, but the sphere of another is beset with fear.†

Bhagvadgitâ.

---

* तदेतदृचाभ्युक्तमेष नित्यो महिमा ब्राह्मणस्य न वर्द्धते कर्मणा नो कनीयान् तस्यैव स्यात्पदवित्तं विदित्वा न लिप्यते कर्मणा पापकेनेति तस्मादेवंविच्छान्तो दान्त उपरतस्तितिक्षुः समाहितो भूत्वात्मन्येवात्मानं पश्यति सर्वमात्मानं पश्यति विपापो विरजोऽविचिकित्सो ब्राह्मणो भवत्येष ब्रह्मलोकः सम्राडिति होवाच याज्ञवल्क्यः ॥

बृहदारण्यकोपनिषत्.

† श्रेयान्स्वधर्मो विगुणः परधर्मात्स्वनुष्ठितात् ॥
स्वधर्मे निधनं श्रेयः परधर्मो भयावहः ॥

भगवद्गीता.

CLXXXIX.

I know this (Self) to be the All, the Great Self, all effulgence, transcending all darkness. Knowing this, one can transcend even death ;—there surely is no other road out of this (world).*

S'vetâśvataropanishad.

CXC.

LIKE and dislike do not cease to affect him who yet relates himself to the body ; these never touch him who has disembodied himself.†

Chhândogyopanishad.

CXCI.

AS oil is found in sesamum-seeds, as *ghee* is found in curds, as water is found in water-courses, or as fire is found in the *araṇi*-wood, so is the Self seen in Self by him who tries to realize it through universal love and perfect control over mind and body.‡

S'vetâśvataropanishad.

---

* वेदाहमेतं पुरुषं महान्त-
मादित्यवर्णं तमसः परस्तात् ।
तमेव विदित्वातिमृत्युमेति
नान्यः पन्था विद्यतेऽयनाय ॥

श्वेताश्वतरोपनिषत्.

† न वै सशरीरस्य सतः प्रियाप्रिययोरपहतिरस्त्यशरीरं वा वसन्तं न प्रियाप्रिये स्पृशतः ॥

छान्दोग्योपनिषत्.

‡ तिलेषु तैलं दधनीव सर्पि-
रापः स्रोतःस्वरणीषु चाग्निः ।
एवमात्मात्मनि गृह्यतेऽसौ-
सत्येनैनं तपसा योऽनुपश्यति

श्वेताश्वतरोपनिषत्.

CXCII.

BRÂHMAṆAS and others desirous of knowing It, know It by the study of the *Veda*, by sacrifice, by ascetic practices unaccompanied with desire ;—knowing It he becomes the silent one.*

Bṛhadâraṇyakopanishad.

CXCIII.

HAVING explained the *Veda* to his pupil, the teacher thus enjoins him: Tell the truth, go by religious forms, never disregard thy proper study, and having satisfied thy teacher with wealth do not put an end to thy line.†

Taittiriyopanishad.

CXCIV.

THREE are the stays of religion :—sacrifice, study, and charity.‡

Chhândogyopanishad.

---

* तमेतं वेदानुवचनेन ब्राह्मणा विविदिषन्ति यज्ञेन दानेन तपसानाशकेनै-तमेव विदित्वा मुनिर्भवति ॥

बृहदारण्यकोपनिषत्.

† वेदमनूच्याचार्योऽन्तेवासिनमनुशास्ति । सत्यं वद । धर्मञ्चर । स्वाध्यायान्मा प्रमदः । आचार्याय प्रियं धनमाहृत्य प्रजातन्तुं मा व्यवच्छेत्सीः ॥

तैत्तिरीयोपनिषत्.

‡ त्रयो धर्मस्कन्धा यज्ञोऽध्ययनं दानमिति ।

छान्दोग्योपनिषत्.

CXCV.

HE who knows It (the immutable *Aumkâra*) thus, and he who does not know It thus, both perform (*Karma*) by It. *Vidyâ* and *Avidyâ* admit of innumerable varieties; that alone which is done with knowledge, faith, and complete surrender, becomes powerful (for good).*

Chhândogyopanishad.

CXCVI—CXCVIII.

THE beautifully-feathered couple bearing the same friendly name squats upon the same tree; one of the pair eats of the tasteful *pippal* (tree), the other looks on without touching anything. The *purusha* bound to this tree, continues to lament, being overpowered to helplessness by the force of delusion, but he passes beyond all sorrow when he sees (his) higher Lord, sought after by all, and experiences the greatness of His glory. When the seeker finds the Lord, the Creator, the Self, the first reflection of *Brahman*, all enveloped in his golden glory, then, indeed, does he, shaking off all good and evil, attain to the height of evenness, being ever unconditioned and unbound.†

Muṇdakopanishad.

---

* तेनोभौ कुरुतो यश्चैतदेवं वेद यश्च न वेद । नाना तु विद्या चाविद्या च यदेव विद्यया करोति श्रद्धयोपनिषदा तदेव वीर्यवत्तरं भवतीति ॥

छान्दोग्योपनिषत्.

† द्वा सुपर्णा सयुजा सखाया समानं वृक्षं परिषस्वजाते ।
तयोरन्यः पिप्पलं स्वाद्वत्त्यनश्नन्नन्योऽभिचाकशीति ॥
समाने वृक्षे पुरुषो निमग्नोऽनीशया शोचति मुह्यमानः ।
जुष्टं यदा पश्यत्यन्यमीशमस्य महिमानमिति वीतशोकः ॥
यदा पश्यः पश्यते रुक्मवर्णं कर्तारमीशं पुरुषं ब्रह्मयोनिम् ।
तदा विद्वान् पुण्यपापे विधूय निरञ्जनः परमं साम्यमुपैति ॥

मुण्डकोपनिषत् .

CXCIX.

THAT wherein are fixed all blood-vessels whatever, even like the radii fixed in the navel of a chariot-wheel, is He, the internal one, pervading everything, and appearing as many (after the forms of the intellect). Meditate on this thy Self as the syllable *Aum*; may you be ever happy in the realization of that which transcends all darkness.*

Muṇdakopanishad.

CC—CCI.

SEEING the whole universe subject to the law of causation, the *Brâhmaṇa* understands that there is nothing which is the causeless uncreate, and finding no use in acting (upto the ideals of the world) feels supreme contempt for everything. He then repairs, with holy grass in hand, to the teacher, well-versed in sacred lore and full of the realization of *Brahman*, to inquire after the Eternal. The knower explains to him who with mind free from all egoism, and with the senses turned within, repairs to him, thus questioning, that *Brahma-idyâ* which reveals the eternal *Purusha*, the highest Truth.†

Muṇdakopanishad.

---

* अरा इव रथनाभौ संहता यत्र नाड्यः ।
स एषोऽन्तश्चरते बहुधा जायमानः ।
ओमित्येवं ध्यायथ आत्मानं स्वस्ति वः पराय तमसः परस्तात् ॥

मुण्डकोपनिषत्.

† परीक्ष्य लोकान् कर्मचितान् ब्राह्मणो निर्वेदमायान्नास्त्यकृतः कृतेन । तद्विज्ञानार्थं स गुरुमेवाभिगच्छेत्समित्पाणिः श्रोत्रियं ब्रह्मनिष्ठम् ॥

तस्मै स विद्वानुपसन्नाय सम्यक् प्रशान्तचित्ताय शमान्विताय ।
येनाक्षरं पुरुषं वेद सत्यं प्रोवाच तां तत्त्वतो ब्रह्मविद्याम् ॥

मुण्डकोपनिषत्.

CCII—CCIII.

THE chief help to self-realization is, however, that reflection which comes of one's own effort ; all the rest, including (the teacher's) grace and so forth are but subordinate means to the end. Attend, therefore, carefully to the principal means. If the teacher can raise the ignorant, without his personal effort, what is there to prevent him from carrying a camel or even an ox, already broken, to the bliss of complete liberation ?*

Yogavâsishtha.

V.—Experience.

CCIV—CCV.

BEYOND desire, without parts, above egoism, being or non-being ;—whatever Thou art, Thou can'st not escape from being the Creator. Thou destroyest, protectest, givest, shinest, speakest, though ever free from egoism ;—wonderful is the power of thy *Mâyâ* (illusion).†

Yogavâsishtha.

---

* मुख्यः पुरुषयत्नोत्थो विचारः स्वात्मदर्शने ।
गौणो वरादिको हेतुर्मुख्यहेतुपरो भव ॥
गुरुश्चेदुद्धरत्यज्ञमात्मीयात्पौरुषादृते ।
उष्ट्रं दांतं बलीवर्दं तत्कस्मान्नोद्धरत्यसौ ॥

योगवासिष्ठम्.

† निरीहेण निरंशेन निरहङ्कृतिना त्वया ।
सता वाप्यसता वापि कर्तृत्वमुररीकृतम् ॥
हंसि पासि ददासि त्वमवस्फूर्जसि वल्गसि ।
अनहंकृतिरूपोऽपि चित्रेयं तव मायिता ॥

योगवासिष्ठम्.

CCVI.

HE felt a desire, I may become many and multiply. He objectified himself and evolved all this, everything whatever. Having evolved this, he entered into it; and entering became all positives and all negatives, ..., all spirit and all matter, all truth and all untruth.*

Taittiriyopanishad.

CCVII.

THEN, It was all unmanifest, It, of itself, became manifest only through name and form, endowing everything with this or that name and this or that form. All things even till now become defined by some name and some form. This is all the import of His "entering" (in the objective evolved from himself).†

Bṛhadâraṇyakopanishad.

---

* सोऽकामयत बहुस्यां प्रजायेयेति । स तपोऽतप्यत । स तपस्तप्त्वेदं सर्वमसृजत । यदिदं किञ्च । तत्सृष्ट्वा तदेवानुप्राविशत् । तदनुप्रविश्य सच्च त्यच्चाभवत् । ...... । विज्ञानञ्चाविज्ञानञ्च । सत्यञ्चानृतञ्च ॥

तैत्तिरीयोपनिषत्.

† तद्धेदं तर्ह्यव्याकृतमासीत्तन्नामरूपाभ्यामेव व्याक्रियतासौनामायमिदंरूप इति तदिदमप्येतर्हि नामरूपाभ्यामेव व्याक्रियतेऽसौनामायमिदंरूप इति स एष इह प्रविष्टः ॥

बृहदारण्यकोपनिषत्.

CCVIII.

DADHYANGÂTHARVAṆA thus described this "honey*" to the Aśvinikumâras; the seer, no doubt, said what he saw, for he described It as taking on a separate form with every form. The ever-effulgent is understood to take on many forms through illusion solely for the purpose of self-realization.†

Bṛhadâraṇyakopanishad.

CCIX.

THE one self-enlightened becoming everything from the highest to the lowest, becomes the many in dream, and as it were, enjoys all pleasures with women, laughs (a hearty laugh with friends), or feels the sense of fear on seeing cause for it.‡

Bṛhadâraṇyakopanishad.

---

* *Brahman* being compared throughout the chapter to the "honey" which fills the comb, and is partaken of individually by every bee in every individual cell.

† इदं वै तन्मधु दध्यङ्ङाथर्वणोऽश्विभ्यामुवाच तदेतदृषिः पश्यन्नवोचद्रूपं रूपं प्रतिरूपो बभूव तदस्य रूपं प्रतिचक्षणाय इन्द्रो मायाभिः पुरुरूप ईयते ॥

बृहदारण्यकोपनिषद्.

‡ स्वप्नान्त उच्चावचमीयमानो ।
रूपाणि देवः कुरुते बहूनि ॥
उतेव स्त्रीभिः सह मोदमानो ।
जक्षदुतेवापि भयानि पश्यन् ॥

बृहदारण्यकोपनिषद्.

CCX.

IN dream there are no chariots, no horses, not even the course on which the chariot may be run; and yet all these are created in a moment. There are no joys, no pleasures, no delights; and yet all are seen and felt at the instant. There are no ponds, no lakes, no rivers; and yet all are there at the merest thought. This power of evolving any number of forms from itself is the Creator.*

Bṛahadâraṇyakopanishad.

CCXI—CCXIII.

THIS, therefore, is the Truth. As from fire well lighted, fiery sparks flow off in all directions by the thousand, so do all beings of every variety come out, oh good one! from the ever Immutable, and are resolved also into the same. It is the self-illumined, formless, *Purusha*, all within and all without, unborn, without breath, without mind, above all conditions, beyond the eternal cause of the phenomenal. From it spring forth breath, mind, and all the senses, nay *Âkâśa*, *Vâyu*, *Tejas*, *Jala*, and *Prithivi*, the sustainer of all.†

Muṇdakopanishad.

---

* न तत्र रथा न रथयोगा न पन्थानो भवन्त्यथ रथान् रथयोगान् पथः सृजते न तत्रानन्दा मुदः प्रमुदो भवन्त्यथानन्दान्मुदः प्रमुदः सृजते न तत्र वेशान्ताः पुष्करिण्यः स्रवन्त्यो भवन्त्यथ वेशान्ताः पुष्करिण्यः स्रवन्त्यः सृजते स हि कर्त्ता ॥

बृहदारण्यकोपनिषत्.

† तदेतत्सत्यम् । यथा सुदीप्तात् पावकाद्विस्फुलिङ्गाः सहस्रशः प्रभवन्ते सरूपाः । तथाक्षराद्विविधाः सोम्य भावाः प्रजायन्ते तत्र चैवापि यन्ति ॥

दिव्यो ह्यमूर्तः पुरुषः सबाह्याभ्यन्तरो ह्यजः ।
अप्राणो ह्यमनाः शुभ्रो ह्यक्षरात्परतः परः ॥
एतस्माज्जायते प्राणो मनः सर्वेन्द्रियाणि च ।
खं वायुर्ज्योतिरापः पृथिवी विश्वस्य धारिणी ॥

मुण्डकोपनिषत्.

CCXIV—CCXV.

CAMPHOR and the like never cease to emit fragrance though kept in any place whatever; the whole of the phenomenal may, in the same manner, be seen in that which is all consciousness. As the bracelet is in the gold, as water is in the mirage, or even as a wall stands round the city seen in dream, so subsists the form of every object in the subject.*

Yogavâsishtha.

CCXVI.

HE who generally knows everything, knows the same particularly also; this omniscience is the only austerity known to him. From him came forth this *Brahman* (*i. e.*, the *Hiraṇyagarbha*), all names, all forms, all nourishment.†

Muṇḍakopanishad.

CCXVII.

AS the statue pre-exists in the wood, and a statue exists again in every limb of that statue, and so on *ad infinitum*, so does this gigantic statue—the Kosmos—(exist in the All).‡

Yogavâsishtha.

---

* यत्र तत्र स्थितस्यापि कर्पूरादेः सुगंधिता ।
यथोदेति तथा दृश्यं चिद्धातोरुदरे जगत् ॥
अङ्गदत्वं यथा हेम्नि मृगनद्यां यथा जलम् ।
भित्तिर्यथा स्वप्नपुरे तथा द्रष्टरि दृश्यधीः ॥

योगवासिष्ठम्.

† यः सर्वज्ञः सर्वविद्यस्य ज्ञानमयं तपः ।
तस्मादेतद्ब्रह्म नामरूपमन्नं च जायते ॥

मुण्डकोपनिषद्.

‡ यथा स्तंभे पुत्रिकान्तास्तस्याः स्वाङ्गेषु पुत्रिका ।
तस्याश्च पुत्रिकास्त्यङ्गे तथा त्रैलोक्यपुत्रिका ॥

योगवासिष्ठम्.

CCXVIII—CCXIX.

THE wise realize everywhere that which is beyond sight, beyond grasp, which has no relation whatever, which has no form, which has no eye and no ear, no hand, no foot, which is eternal, all-pervading, smallest of the small, ever immutable, the source of all being. As a spider spins out his web from within himself and draws it in (at pleasure), or as herbs grow out of the earth, or as hairs grow out of the living man, so, indeed, does evolve the Kosmos from the ever unchangeable (All).*

Muṇḍakopanishad.

CCXX—CCXXII.

THIS *Aśvattha*-tree, with root upward and branches extending below, stands eternally thriving; it is the spotless, it is *Brahman*, that verily is the Immortal; all worlds subsist in It, nothing can transcend It. This is That. Through his fear burns fire, through his fear shines the sun, through His fear thunders Indra, through His fear blows the wind, nay through His fear runs to duty the fifth—death. If

---

* यत्तदद्रेश्यमग्राह्यमगोत्रमवर्ण-
मचक्षुःश्रोत्रं तदपाणिपादम् ।
नित्यं विभुं सर्वगतं सुसूक्ष्मं
तदव्ययं यद्भूतयोनिं परिपश्यन्ति धीराः ।
यथोर्णनाभिः सृजते गृह्णते च
यथा पृथिव्यामोषधयः सम्भवन्ति ।
यथा सतः पुरुषात् केशलोमानि
तथाक्षरात् सम्भवतीह विश्वम् ॥

मुण्डकोपनिषत्.

thou failest in this (world) to see the Light before the dissolution of thy body, thou hast before thee a passage in (another body) through worlds and creations.*

Kathopanishad.

CCXXIII.

As consciousness bears witness to itself, or as separateness bears out separateness, so is illusion sufficient, of itself, to bear out itself and everything it contains. This indeed is *Mâyâ*, capable of bringing about things and events beyond conception;—it deludes all in the whirl of its illusive action.†

Svârâjyasiddhi.

---

* ऊर्ध्वमूलोऽवाक्शाख एषोऽश्वत्थः सनातनः ।
तदेव शुक्रं तद्ब्रह्म तदेवामृतमुच्यते ।
तस्मिल्लोकाः श्रिताः सर्वे तदु नात्येति कश्चन ॥ एतद्वै तत् ॥
भयादस्याग्निस्तपति भयात्तपति सूर्यः ।
भयादिन्द्रश्च वायुश्च मृत्युर्धावति पञ्चमः ॥
कठोपनिषत् । बृहदारण्यकोपनिषत् । तैत्तिरीयोपनिषत् .
इह चेदशकद्बोद्धुं प्राक् शरीरस्य विस्रसः ।
ततः सर्गेषु लोकेषु शरीरत्वाय कल्पते ॥
कठोपनिषत् .

† चिद्भाने चितिरिव या भिदेव भेदे ।
निर्वाहे निजपरयोः स्वतः समर्था ॥
सम्भाव्येतरघटनापटीयसी सा ।
संमोहं जनयति विभ्रमेण माया ॥
स्वाराज्यसिद्धिः

CCXXIV—CCXXV.

THE self-existent inflicted a curse on the senses in endowing them with a tendency to objectivize; it is hence that they tend to objects without, and not to the subject within. Some rare sage desirous of immortality sees the Self, turning his eyes within. Children find pleasure in the objective, and become bound in the expansive net of death ; the wise knowing immortality as the only thing stable, care not to desire anything of the impermanent.*

Kathopanishad.

CCXXVI—CCXXXII.

REAPING the fruit of their own action in this world, resting in the cavity of the heart—the other half of the Supreme—these two (*Jiva* and *Brahman*) are described after the illustration of light and darkness, by the knowers of *Brahman*, nay by those householders who worship the five fires, as also by those who keep the three *Nâchiketa*-fires. That *Nâchiketa*-fire, the bridge over which pass worshippers desirous of crossing over to the other side, and that which is *Brahman* the immutable Supreme, beyond all fear, we have

---

* पराञ्चि खानि व्यतृणत्स्वयम्भू-
स्तस्मात्पराङ् पश्यति नान्तरात्मन् ।
कश्चिद्धीरः प्रत्यगात्मानमैक्ष-
दावृत्तचक्षुरमृतत्वमिच्छन् ॥
पराचः कामाननु यन्ति बाला-
स्ते मृत्योर्यन्ति विततस्य पाशम् ।
अथ धीरा अमृतत्वं विदित्वा
ध्रुवमध्रुवेष्विह न प्रार्थयन्ते ॥

कठोपनिषत्.

certainly been able thus to know. Self is the rider on the chariot of this body guided by the intellect as charioteer, drawn by the senses as powerful horses, controlled by way of the mind serving for the reigns. Thus runs the vehicle over the course of experience. The Self thus conditioned by the senses and the mind is called the enjoyer (the subjective soul—*Jiva*) by those who know. He who is forsaken by the charioteer (intelligent discrimination), and has no idea of guiding the reigns—his mind—in the proper manner, has no control over the senses, like a driver over restive horses. He who has the intellect for his driver and the mind for proper reigns, is able to reach the other end of the course, the highest essence of the all-pervading. This, ever concealed in all, is never manifest, but is grasped by the sharp intellect of those who are trained to minute observation.*

Kathopanishad.

---

* ऋतं पिबन्तौ सुकृतस्य लोके
गुहाम्प्रविष्टौ परमे परार्धे ।
छायातपौ ब्रह्मविदो वदन्ति
पञ्चाग्नयो ये च त्रिणाचिकेताः ॥
यः सेतुरीजानानामक्षरम्ब्रह्म यत्परम् ।
अभयं तितीर्षताम्पारं नाचिकेतं शकेमहि ॥
आत्मानं रथिनं विद्धि शरीरं रथमेव तु ।
बुद्धिन्तु सारथिम्विद्धि मनः प्रग्रहमेव च ॥
इन्द्रियाणि हयानाहुर्विषयाँस्तेषु गोचरान् ।
आत्मेन्द्रियमनोयुक्तं भोक्तेत्याहुर्मनीषिणः ॥
यस्त्वविज्ञानवान् भवत्ययुक्तेन मनसा सदा ।
तस्येन्द्रियाण्यवश्यानि दुष्टाश्वा इव सारथेः ॥
विज्ञानसारथिर्यस्तु मनःप्रग्रहवान्नरः ।
सोऽध्वनः पारमाप्नोति तद्विष्णोः परमं पदम् ॥
एष सर्वेषु भूतेषु गूढोत्मा न प्रकाशते ।
दृश्यते त्वग्र्यया बुध्या सूक्ष्मया सूक्ष्मदर्शिभिः ॥

कठोपनिषत्.

CCXXXIII—CCXXXIV.

THOUGH having only three *guṇas* (forms), thou* art the cause of all the worlds ; even Hari and Hara and other gods fail, through want of insight, to measure the depth of thy immeasurable power. Thou art the sustainer of all, the whole of this universe is only a particle of thyself ;—thou indeed art the undifferenced first cause, the highest *Prakṛti.* Oh divine mother ! thou art that supreme science (*Vidyâ*), of power inconceivably immense, which sages desirous of liberation, rising above every weakness, apply themselves to, with the inner power of their senses held tight in perfect control.†

The Saptaśati (*Mârkendeyapurâṇa*).

CCXXXV.

THOU art the light that shines through the sun dispelling the darkness of ignorance (*Avidyâ*) prevailing within ; thou art the vein that carries the fragrant honey of the flower of consciousness to every particle of matter ; thou art that which becomes a thousand of that jewel which satisfies every

---

* *Mâyâ-S'akti*, the principle of energy underlying all evolution.

† हेतुः समस्तजगतां त्रिगुणापि दोषै-
र्न ज्ञायसे हरिहरादिभिरप्यपारा ।
सर्वाश्रयाखिलमिदं जगदंशभूत-
मव्याकृता हि परमा प्रकृतिस्त्वमाद्या ॥
या मुक्तिहेतुरविचिन्त्यमहाव्रता त्व-
मभ्यस्यसे सुनियतेन्द्रियतत्त्वसारैः ।
मोक्षार्थिभिर्मुनिभिरस्तसमस्तदोषै-
र्विद्यासि सा भगवती परमा हि देवि ॥

सप्तशती.

desire of the needy ; thou, divine one ! art to those struggling in the ocean of incarnation, the tusk of that boar who was the enemy of the giant Mura.†*

Ânandalahari.

CCXXXVI.

THIS divine godess, the power of supreme illusion (*Mahâmâyâ*), forcibly drags away the mind even of the knower into the web of delusion.†

Saptaśati (Mârkandeyapurâṇa).

CCXXXVII.

HE who while fully anxious of his body, desires to realize Self, prepares to cross a river on the back of a crocodile mistaking it for a piece of wood.‡

Vivekachudâmaṇi.

---

† The giant Mura is fabled to have carried the earth into the ocean, and the god Vishṇu, taking the form of a boar, raised the earth on his tusk, and established her in position.

* अविद्यानामन्तस्तिमिरमिहिरोद्दीपनकरी
जडानां चैतन्यस्तबकमकरन्दस्रुतिशिरा ।
दरिद्राणां चिन्तामणिगुणनिका जन्मजलधौ
निमग्नानां दंष्ट्रा मुररिपुवराहस्य भवती ॥

आनन्दलहरी.

† ज्ञानिनामपि चेतांसि देवी भगवती हि सा ।
बलादाकृष्य मोहाय महामाया प्रयच्छति ॥

सप्तशती.

‡ शरीरपोषणार्थी सन् य आत्मानं दिदृक्षति ।
ग्राहं दारुधिया धृत्वा नदीं तर्तुं स गच्छति ॥

विवेकचूडामणिः

CCXXXVIII—CCXXXIX.

FINDING even the knower lean towards objects and enjoyments, forgetfulness throws him off the guard, like an adulteress her paramour, by clouding his intellect. As moss moved from upon the face of water stands not away even for a minute, delusion (*Mâyâ*) envelopes even the knowing one, if he is off his guard.*

Vivekachudâmaṇi.

CCXL.

WIFE, daughter-in-law, sister-in-law, brother's wife, mother, and so on, does the same woman appear on account of the counter-entities she is made to represent;—she herself continues ever one.†

Panchadaśi.

---

* विषयाभिमुखं दृष्ट्वा विद्वांसमपि विस्मृतिः ।
विक्षेपयति धीदोषैर्योषा जारमिव प्रियम् ॥
यथापकृष्टं शैवालं क्षणमात्रं न तिष्ठति ॥
आवृणोति तथा माया प्राज्ञं वापि पराङ्मुखम् ॥

विवेकचूडामणिः.

† भार्या स्नुषा ननान्दा च याता मातेत्यनेकधा ।
प्रातियोगिधिया योषिद्भिद्यते न स्वरूपतः ॥

पञ्चदशी.

CCXLI.

THAT the origin of experience is explained from evolution, after the manner of (pots, etc., from) clay, (instruments etc., from) iron, or sparks (from fire), and so on, is only a method of putting (the matter to the learner); there is, in reality, no distinction whatever (in the All).*

Gaudapâdâchârya.

CCXLII.

HE, who imagines a limit in the limitless, transcendant, Self, has, of himself, put his self in bondage.†

Yogavâsishtha.

CCXLIII.

THAT which is naught at beginning and end, is naught in the present moment also; (things) though fully resembling unreality, are said to be real by, as it were, a kind of metaphor.‡

Gaudapâdâchârya.

CCXLIV.

THIS illusion of Mine made up of the (three) *gunas* (forms of the intellect) is intransgressible;—those who betake themselves to Me, cross over to the other side of the stream.§

Bhagavadgitâ.

---

* मृल्लोहविस्फुलिङ्गाद्यैः सृष्टिर्या चोदितान्यथा ।
उपायः सोऽवताराय नास्ति भेदः कथञ्चन ॥
गौडपादाचार्याः.

† अनंतस्याप्रमेयस्य येनेयत्ता प्रकल्पिता ।
आत्मनस्तस्य तेनात्मा स्वात्मनैव वशीकृतः ॥
योगवासिष्ठम्.

‡ आदावन्ते च यन्नास्ति वर्त्तमानेऽपि तत्तथा ।
वितथैः सदृशाः सन्तोऽवितथा इव लक्षिताः ॥
गौडपादाचार्याः

§ दैवी ह्येषा गुणमयी मम माया दुरत्यया ।
मामेवानुप्रपद्यन्ते मायामेतां तरन्ति ते ॥
भगवद्गीता.

CCXLV.

EXPERIENCE known as *experience* tends to degrade, but known as import of the Word, *Brahman*, it becomes all perfect bliss.*

Yogavâsishtha.

CCXLVI.

FEAR comes of attachment to duality, in him who, being removed from the Lord, is overpowered, through His illusion, with false imaginations and forgetfulness (of self-identity). It therefore beloves the thoughtful, one with the teacher as his supreme lord, to lose himself in entire devotion.†

Bhâgavata.

CCXLVII.

THOU alone eternally evolvest through the gracefulness of thyself made up of being and non-being, having for its embodiment the wonderful variety of endless objects.‡

Yogavâsishtha.

---

* सर्गस्तु सर्गशब्दार्थतया बुद्धो नयत्यधः ।
स ब्रह्मशब्दार्थतया बुद्धः श्रेयोमवत्यलम् ॥

योगवासिष्ठम्.

† भयं द्वितीयाभिनिवेशतः स्या-
दीशादपेतस्य विपर्ययोऽस्मृतिः ।
तन्माययातो बुध आभजेत्तं
भक्त्यैकयेशं गुरुदेवतात्मा ॥

भागवतम्.

‡ त्वमेवानन्तयानन्तवस्तुवैचित्र्यरूपया ।
भावाभावविलासिन्या नित्ययैव विजृम्भसे ॥

योगवासिष्ठम्.

CCXLVIII.

AS the rope, not understood as such, is mistaken, in the dark, for a snake or a line of water, and the like, so is *Âtman* (mistaken for the variety of this world).*

Gaudapâdâchârya.

CCXLIX.

EXPERIENCE, full of likes and dislikes, is verily a dream; real while it lasts, all unreal on being awake.†

Âtmabodha.

---

vi.—Karma.

CCL.

FORTITUDE, forbearance, self-restraint, no desire for other's wealth, purity, control over the senses, conscious intelligence, (spiritual) culture, truthfulness, absence of anger,—these ten make up the characteristics of all true religion whatever.‡

Manu.

---

* अनिश्चिता यथा रज्जुरन्धकारे विकल्पिता ।
सर्पधारादिभिर्भावैस्तद्वदात्मा विकल्पितः ॥

गौडपादाचार्यः

† संसारः स्वप्नतुल्यो हि रागद्वेषादिसंकुलः ।
स्वकाले सत्यवद्भाति प्रबोधे सत्यसद्भवेत् ॥

आत्मबोधः

‡ धृतिः क्षमा दमोऽस्तेयं शौचमिन्द्रियनिग्रहः ।
धीर्विद्या सत्यमक्रोधो दशकं धर्मलक्षणम् ॥

मनुः

CCLI—CCLII.

As the caterpillar, getting to the end of the straw, takes itself away only after finding a resting-place in advance, so this *Átman* leaving this body, and finding another place in advance, through *Avidyá*, takes himself off from his original abode. As the goldsmith taking little by little of the gold expands it into a new form, so, indeed, does this *Átman*, leaving this body, make a new and happy abode for himself, passing through *Avidyá*, and takes on the form of the *Pitṛs*, or the *Gandharvas*, or the gods, or *Prajápati*, or *Brahmá*, or any other being whatever.*

Bṛhadáraṇyakopanishad.

CCLIII—CCLIV.

The sacrifice which the eighteen† partake in is all inferior *Karma*, it drowns itself and those who betake themselves to it. Those fools who imagine any good in this, are led again and again into the wheel of decay and death. Those men of stupid intellect who imagine *S'rauta* and *Smárta*

---

* तद्यथा तृणजलायुका तृणस्यान्तं गत्वान्यमाक्रममाक्रम्यात्मानमुपसंहरत्येव-मेवायमात्मेदं शरीरं निहत्याविद्यां गमयित्वान्यमाक्रममाक्रम्यात्मानमुपसंहरति ॥

तद्यथा पेशस्कारी पेशसो मात्रामुपादायान्यन्नवतरं कल्याणतरं रूपं तनुत एवमेवायमात्मेदं शरीरं निहत्याविद्यां गमयित्वान्यन्नवतरं कल्याणतरं रूपं कुरुते पित्र्यं वा गान्धर्वं वा दैवं वा प्राजापत्यं वा ब्राह्मं वान्येषां वा भूतानाम् ॥

बृहदारण्यकोपनिषत्.

† Sixteen priests, the master of the house and his wife, make up the eighteen.

Karma as the height of religion, and know no good besides, attain to heaven, and having lived out their good *Karma*, return again into this world or even into a lower one.*

Muṇḍakopanishad.

CCLV.

THE Vedas deal with the three *Guṇas*; Oh Arjuna! rise above the *Guṇas*, shake off all duality, be ever centred in supreme peace, abandon all anxiety for acquisition or protection, and above all know thy Self.†

Bhagavadgitâ.

CCLVI.

THEREFORE as here, in this world, dies out what may be encompassed by *action*, so is put out in the world next to this, all that may be acquired through acts of formal religion.‡

Chhândogyopanishad.

---

* प्लवा ह्येते अदृढा यज्ञरूपा अष्टादशोक्तमवरं येषु कर्म।
एतच्छ्रेयो येऽभिनन्दन्ति मूढा जरामृत्युं ते पुनरेवापि यन्ति॥
इष्टापूर्तं मन्यमाना वरिष्ठं नान्यच्छ्रेयो वेदयन्ते प्रमूढाः।
नाकस्य पृष्ठे ते सुकृतेऽनुभूत्वेमं लोकं हीनतरञ्चाविशन्ति॥

मुण्डकोपनिषद्.

† त्रैगुण्यविषया वेदा निस्त्रैगुण्यो भवार्जुन।
निर्द्वन्द्वो नित्यसत्त्वस्थो निर्योगक्षेम आत्मवान्॥

भगवद्गीता.

‡ तद्यथेह कर्म्मजितो लोकः क्षीयत एवमेवामुत्र पुण्यजितो लोकः क्षीयते॥

छान्दोग्योपनिषद्.

CCLVII.

FORMS of religion but forge so many bonds round the individual ; *gnosis* alone disperses them.*

Mahâ-Bhârata.

CCLVIII.

FORMAL religion has its use in purification of the intellect, it cannot show the Thing. The Thing is realized through reflection, not at all even by a million forms of worship.†

Vivekachudâmaṇi.

CCLIX.

KARMAN leads to that result alone which it can produce, reach, evolve, or modify ; liberation is not brought about in any of these ways ; hence *Karman* cannot be the means of liberation.‡

Naishkarmyasiddhi.

---

* कर्मणा बद्ध्यते जन्तुर्विद्यया च विमुच्यते ॥

महाभारतम्.

† चित्तस्य शुद्धये कर्म्म न तु वस्तूपलब्धये ।
वस्तुसिद्धिर्विचारेण न किञ्चित् कर्म्मकोटिभिः ॥

विवेकचूडामणिः.

‡ उत्पाद्यमाप्यं संस्कार्यं विकार्यं च क्रियाफलम् ।
नैवं मुक्तिर्यतस्तस्मात्कर्म तस्या न साधनम् ॥

नैष्कर्म्यसिद्धिः.

CCLX.

KARMAN never dispels ignorance, being under the same category. Knowledge alone destroys ignorance, even as light dispels darkness.*

Âtmabodha.

CCLXI.

OH Dhananjaya! Fulfil every act, being ever centred in *Yoga*, abandoning all attachment whatever; stand even in success or defeat, for this evenness alone is true *Yoga.*†

Bhagavadgitâ.

CCLXII.

HAPPINESS or misery is not in any one's giving, it is all a misunderstanding of the intellect which shows either the one or the other as coming from some one else. Nay, the proud egoism even in the act, of the form 'I do it,' is entirely vain. Every individual is governed by *his own Karman.*‡

Miscellaneous.

---

* अविरोधितया कर्म नाविद्यां विनिवर्त्तयेत् ।
विद्याविद्यां निहन्त्येव तेजस्तिमिरसंघवत् ॥

आत्मबोधः.

† योगस्थः कुरु कर्माणि सङ्गं त्यक्त्वा धनञ्जय ॥
सिद्ध्यसिद्ध्योः समो भूत्वा समत्वं योग उच्यते ॥

भगवद्गीता.

‡ सुखस्य दुःखस्य न कोऽपि दाता
परो ददातीति कुबुद्धिरेषा ।
अहङ्करोमीति मुधाभिमानः
स्वकर्मसूत्रग्रथितो हि लोकः ॥

प्रास्ताविकः

CCLXIII.

THUS, therefore, remaining all unaffected, attend continually to every act which is part of thy duty; the soul doing all acts whatever with supreme non-attachment realizes the highest (Self).*

Bhagavadgitá.

CCLXIV.

HE who sees inaction in action, and action in inaction, is, of all men, the really wise, the true ascetic,—he has fulfilled all acts whatever.†

Bhagavadgitá.

---

vii.—Upa'sana'.

CCLXV.

ALL this verily is *Brahman*, for it is *of* it, *in* it, and *through* it. The self-controlled should devote himself to this *Brahman* (in any way he likes). The man is all Idea,

---

* तस्मादसक्तः सततं कार्यं कर्म समाचर ।
असक्तो ह्याचरन्कर्म परमाप्नोति पूरुषः ॥

भगवद्गीता.

† कर्मण्यकर्म यः पश्येदकर्मणि च कर्म यः ।
स बुद्धिमान्मनुष्येषु स युक्तः कृत्स्नकर्मकृत् ॥

भगवद्गीता.

whatever Idea the man cherishes in this world that he becomes in the next. Fix thyself, therefore, on the Idea.*

Chhândogyopanishad.

CCLXVI.

OH son of Kunti! he becomes that, filling his memory with which, at the last moment, he gives up the body;—being led to it by force of the constant fixing of his mind on that idea.†

Bhagavadgitâ.

CCLXVII.

A Collection of water is not all that makes a holy place, a lump of earth or stone is not all that makes a God;—these purify after much length of time, the good exhalt by mere sight.‡

Bhâgavata.

---

* सर्वं खल्विदं ब्रह्म तज्जलानिति शान्त उपासीत ॥
अथ खलु क्रतुमयः पुरुषो यथा क्रतुरस्मिँल्लोके पुरुषो
भवति तथेतः प्रेत्य भवति स क्रतुं कुर्वीत ॥

छान्दोग्योपनिषत्.

† यं यं वापि स्मरन्भावं त्यजत्यन्ते कलेवरम् ।
तं तमेवैति कौन्तेय सदा तद्भावभावितः ॥

भगवद्गीता.

‡ न ह्यम्मयानि तीर्थानि न देवा मृच्छिलामयाः ।
ते पुनन्त्युरुकालेन दर्शनादेव साधवः ॥

भागवतम्.

CCLXVIII.

TEACHERS, interpretations of sacred texts, the force of religious merit, none of these lead to the realization of that condition which is revealed in the clear reflection of the heart engendered from contact with the good.*

Yogavâsishtha.

CCLXIX—CCLXX.

CLARIFIED butter though present in every limb of the cow conduces naught to her nourishment; it serves as the best medicine to its producer on being worked out into its proper form. In the same manner, the highest effulgent Lord, present in all beings, even like the clarified butter, is never of any practical use to them, till properly realized through the force of devotion.†

Yogavâsishtha.

---

* न तद्गुरोर्न शास्त्रार्थान्न पुण्यात्प्राप्यते पदम् ।
यत्साधुसङ्गाभ्युदिताद्विचारविशदाद्धृदः ॥

योगवासिष्ठम्.

† गवां सर्पिः शरीरस्थं न करोत्यङ्गपोषणम् ।
तदेव कर्मरचितं पुनस्तस्यैव भेषजम् ॥
एवं सर्वशरीरस्थः सर्पिर्वत्परमेश्वरः ।
विना चोपासनां देवो न करोति हितं नृषु ॥

योगवासिष्ठम्.

CCLXXI—CCLXXII.

IF you ask what can be the difference between Gnosis and devotion? pray hear; reflection is bound up with the *thing*, devotion with the *actor*. Gnosis comes of reflection, no opposite desire can put it out; it burns up every trace of reality in the world of phenomena, in the very moment of its birth.*

Panchadaśi.

CCLXXIII.

THIS body is the holy Kâśi; the river of Gnosis flowing through and through the three worlds is the sacred Ganges; devotion and faith stand for the heavenly Gayâ; the much-coveted Prayâga is, indeed, in deep concentration on the feet of the teacher; and this inner Self, the fourth, the witness of every one's mind, is the God Viśveśvara;—if thus all holy places stand together in this body of mine, what other place could be holier to seek?†

Kâśi-panchaka.

---

* बोधोपास्त्योर्विशेषः क इति चेदुच्यते शृणु ।
वस्तुतन्त्रो भवेद्बोधः कर्तृतन्त्रमुपासनम् ॥
विचाराज्जायते बोधोऽनिच्छा यं न निवर्तयेत् ।
स्वोत्पत्तिमात्रात्संसारे दहत्यखिलसत्यताम् ॥

पञ्चदशी.

† काशीक्षेत्रं शरीरं त्रिभुवनजठरे व्यापिनी ज्ञानगंगा
भक्तिः श्रद्धा गयेयं निजगुरुचरणध्यानयोगः प्रयागः ।
विश्वेशोऽयं तुरीयः सकलजनमनः साक्षिभूतोऽन्तरात्मा
देहे सर्वं मदीये यदि वसति पुनस्तीर्थमन्यत्किमस्ति ॥

काशीपञ्चकम्.

CCLXXIV.

FORMAL objects of worship are devised for the use of those who have not yet realized the essence of Beneficience; going by miles is devised for those who cannot go by leagues.*

Yogavâsishtha.

CCLXXV.

I am even to all beings, I do neither dislike nor like any one:—those who resign themselves to me with entire devotion, are in me, and I am in them.†

Bhagavadgitâ.

CCLXXVI.

SAID Prajâpati: whence does come this fear! with the thought, 'why did I fear?' disappeared all fear; for, fear comes of duality.‡

Bṛhadâraṇyakopanishad.

---

* अज्ञातशिवतत्त्वानामाकाराद्यर्चनं कृतम् ।
योजनाध्वन्यशक्तस्य क्रोशाध्वा परिकल्पते ॥

योगवासिष्ठम्.

† समोऽहं सर्वभूतेषु न मे द्वेष्योऽस्ति न प्रियः ।
ये भजन्ति तु मां भक्त्या मयि ते तेषु चाप्यहम् ॥

भगवद्गीता.

‡ कस्मान्नु बिभेमीति तत एवास्य भयं वीयाय
कस्माद्ध्यभेष्यद् द्वितीयाद्वै भयम्भवति ॥

बृहदारण्यकोपनिषत्.

CCLXXVII.

INSIST not on the order (of steps in the process of Self-realization); the inverted vision which, like hunger, is the cause of much tangible suffering, must in one way or other, be cured.*

Panchadaśi.

CCLXXVIII.

ATTEND to this, the essence of all *Gnosis*, and attending, digest it well:—Desire alone is bondage, its destruction is liberation.†

Yogavâsishtha.

CCLXXIX.

TO all ascetics whatever, the condition of fearlessness depends upon control of the mind, which leads also to destruction of misery, perfect light, and inexhaustible peace.‡

Gaudapâdâchârya.

---

* क्षुधेव दृष्टबाधाकृद्विपरीता च भावना ।
ज्ञेया केनाप्युपायेन नास्त्यत्रानुष्ठितेः क्रमः ॥

पञ्चदशी.

† श्रूयतां ज्ञानसर्वस्वं श्रुत्वा चैवावधार्यताम् ।
भोगेच्छामात्रको बन्धस्तत्त्यागो मोक्ष उच्यते ॥

योगवासिष्ठम्.

‡ मनसो निग्रहायत्तमभयं सर्वयोगिनाम् ।
दुःखक्षयः प्रबोधश्चाप्यक्षया शान्तिरेव च ॥

श्रीगौडपादाचार्याः.

CCLXXX.

THAT oh Râma! is the mind which is between being and non-being, which stands between spirit and matter, which in fact swings to and fro between the two.*

Yogavâsishtha.

CCLXXXI.

THINKING evolves the objective, all the three worlds exist in and through thinking, the Kosmos melts away on its dissolution. This thinking should carefully be diagnosed.†

Yogavâsishtha.

CCLXXXII.

ALL ideas come of thinking, they disappear on suspension of thinking. Attune this thinking, therefore, to the highest Self, thy inner consciousness.‡

Vivekachudâmaṇi.

---

* यत्तत्सदसतोर्मध्यं यन्मध्यं चित्त्वजाड्ययोः ।
तन्मनः प्रोच्यते राम द्वयोर्दोलायिताकृति ॥

योगवासिष्ठम्.

† चित्तं कारणमर्थानां तस्मिन्सति जगत्त्रयम् ।
तस्मिन्क्षीणे जगत्क्षीणं तच्चिकित्स्यं प्रयत्नतः ॥

योगवासिष्ठम्.

‡ चित्तमूलो विकल्पोऽयं चित्ताभावे न कश्चन ।
अतश्चित्तं समाधेहि प्रत्यग्रूपे परात्मनि ॥

विवेकचूडामणिः.

CCLXXXIII.

THAT which leads to false vision, sets up the *Anâtman* in place of *Átman*, shadows forth a thing in no-thing;—this oh Râghava! is that which we describe as 'thinking'.*

Yogavâsishtha.

CCLXXXIV.

ABANDON all latent desire for the multitude of enjoyments (pressing round), nay give up even the desire for life (as represented in the body), and finally rise above all sense of being and non-being. Find thus full bliss in absolute trance.†

Yogavâsishtha.

CCLXXXV.

'LATENT desire' may be described as that indiscriminate hankering after things which is forgetful of antecedence and consequence on account of the overpowering impression they produce.‡

Yogavâsishtha.

---

* असम्यग्दर्शनं यस्मादनात्मन्यात्मभावनम् ।
यदवस्तुनि वस्तुत्वं तच्चित्तं विद्धि राघव ॥

योगवासिष्ठम्.

† भोगौघवासनां त्यक्त्वा त्यज त्वं देहवासनाम् ।
भावाभावौ ततस्त्यक्त्वा निर्विकल्पः सुखी भव ॥

योगवासिष्ठम्.

‡ दृढभावनया त्यक्तपूर्वापरविचारणम् ।
यदादानं पदार्थस्य वासना सा प्रकीर्तिता ॥

योगवासिष्ठम्.

CCLXXXVI.

MY mind was occupied elsewhere, and I did not see; my mind was occupied elsewhere, and I did not hear; it is through the mind alone that one sees or hears; love, thought, doubt, belief, unbelief, patience, impatience, intelligence, shame, fear, all make up the mind.*

Bṛhadâraṇyakopanishad.

CCLXXXVII.

MIND alone is, to men, the cause of bondage or liberation;—lost in enjoyment it leads to bondage, emptied of the objective it leads to liberation.†

Panchadaśi.

CCLXXXVIII.

THE light of *Gnosis* breaks not in full force upon that puny thing which is all beclouded with fear of the world, with pride of learning, and with love of life.‡

Smṛti.

---

* अन्यत्रमना अभूवन्नादर्शमन्यत्रमना अभूवं नाश्रौषमिति मनसा ह्येव पश्यति मनसा शृणोति कामः सङ्कल्पो विचिकित्सा श्रद्धाश्रद्धा धृतिरधृतिर्ह्रीर्धीर्भीरित्येतत्सर्वं मन एव ॥

बृहदारण्यकोपनिषत्.

† मन एव मनुष्याणां कारणं बन्धमोक्षयोः ।
बन्धाय विषयासक्तं मुक्तौ निर्विषयं स्मृतम् ॥

पञ्चदशी.

‡ लोकवासनया जन्तोः शास्त्रवासनयापि च ।
देहवासनया ज्ञानं यथावन्नैव जायते ॥

स्मृतिः.

CCLXXXIX—CCXC.

THE father, being victim of some cheat, bewails the loss of his son, taking him for dead, though he be full of life in some far off land. On the other hand, he does not bewail even though his son be dead, till the information has not reached him. It is plain, the cause of bondage lies in the mental creation of *being*.*

Panchadaśi.

CCXCI.

YOU may drink the ocean dry, you may uproot from its base the mountain Meru, you may swallow fire, but difficult than all these, oh Good One! is control over the mind.†

Panchadaśi.

CCXCII.

AS fire, not fed by fuel, subsides into its place, so, indeed, does all thinking die out into its source, on not being led into modifications of any kind.‡

In the Jivanmuktiviveka.

---

* दूरदेशं गते पुत्रे जीवत्येवात्र तत्पिता ।
विप्रलम्भकवाक्येन मृतं मत्वा प्ररोदिति ॥
मृतेऽपि तस्मिन्वार्तायां न श्रुतायां न रोदिति ।
अतःसर्वस्य जीवस्य बन्धकृन्मानसं जगत् ॥

पञ्चदशी.

† अप्यब्धिपानान्महतः सुमेरून्मूलनादपि ।
अपि वह्न्यशनात्साधो विषमश्चित्तनिग्रहः ॥

पञ्चदशी.

‡ यथा निरिन्धनो वन्हिः स्वयोनावुपशाम्यति ।
तथा वृत्तिक्षयाच्चित्तं स्वयोनावुपशाम्यति ॥

जीवन्मुक्तिविवेके:.

CCXCIII—CCXCVI.

HE who understanding the mind applies himself, again and again, to subduing it, gains no success without the help of some consummate plan, even like one who fails to subdue a mad elephant without the iron hook. Application to spiritual science, company of the good, abandonment of latent desire, restraining the flow of breath, these are some of the most useful means to control the mind. Those who, in face of these, try to control it through physical practices, lose sight of the lamp, while vainly dispelling darkness with darkness.*

Yogavâsishtha.

CCXCVII.

RENOUNCE all conformity with the world, give up all concern of the body, nay, have nothing to do with the forms of religion and learning ;—thus wear off the false illusion that wraps thy-Self.†

Vivekachudâmaṇi.

---

* उपविश्योपविश्यैव चित्तज्ञेन मुहुर्मुहुः ।
न शक्यते मनो जेतुं विना युक्तिमनिन्दिताम् ॥
अङ्कुशेन विना मत्तो यथा दुष्टमतङ्गजः ।
अध्यात्मविद्याधिगमः साधुसङ्गम एव च ॥
वासनासंपरित्यागः प्राणस्पन्दनिरोधनम् ।
एतास्ता युक्तयः पुष्टाः सन्ति चित्तजये किल ॥
सतीष्वेतासु युक्तिषु हठान्नियमयन्ति ये ।
चेतस्ते दीपमुत्सृज्य विनिघ्नन्ति तमोऽञ्जनैः ॥

योगवासिष्ठम्.

† लोकानुवर्त्तनं त्यक्त्वा त्यक्त्वा देहानुवर्त्तनम् ।
शास्त्रानुवर्तनं त्यक्त्वा स्वाध्यासापनयं कुरु ॥

विवेकचूडामणिः.

CCXCVIII.

AS one desirous of coming out successful in debate applies himself closely to the study of poems, plays, logic and the like, so must he who desires liberation *reflect* constantly on himself.*

Panchadaśi.

CCXCVIX.

THE God of the twice-born is Fire ; the God of the Silent one is his Heart ;——poor intellects find their God in idols ; the even-eyed enlightened one sees God everywhere.†

Uttaragitâ.

---

viii.—Free-will.

CCC—CCCI.

THAT mean spirit should be avoided from a distance, who, relying on the unseen (Fate), attributes his conduct to the unreal and false idea of some one necessitating it from behind. He is verily a beast, constantly in another's power, who thinks he goes to heaven or hell as God may will it.‡

Yogavâsishtha.

---

* काव्यनाटकतर्कादीनभ्यस्यति निरन्तरम् ।
विजिगीषुर्यथा तद्वन्मुमुक्षुः स्वं विचारयेत् ॥

पञ्चदशी.

† अग्निर्देवो द्विजातीनां मुनीनां हृदि दैवतम् ।
प्रतिमास्वल्पबुद्धीनां सर्वत्र समदर्शिनाम् ॥

उत्तरगीता.

‡ कश्चिन्मां प्रेरयत्येवमित्यनर्थकुकल्पने ।
यः स्थितोऽदृष्टमुत्सृज्य त्याज्योऽसौ दूरतोऽधमः ॥
ईश्वरप्रेरितो गच्छेत्स्वर्गं नरकमेव वा ।
स सदैव पराधीनः पशुरेव न संशयः ॥

योगवासिष्ठम्.

CCCII.

EVEN the body being of illusion, where could there be any room for necessity? That the *Srutis* speak of necessity, is only for the enlightenment of the ignorant.*

Aparokshânubhuti.

CCCIII.

IN this world, oh child of the Raghus! every one can always compass everything through well-directed (*i. e.* free) personal effort.†

Yogavâsishtha.

CCCIV.

RESORT to (free) personal effort, hear such word of scripture as points out some useful line of action; the rest, even though as old as time, should be overlooked, with the eye ever fixed on truth and truth alone.‡

Yogavâsishtha.

---

* देहस्यापि प्रपञ्चत्वात्प्रारब्धावस्थितिः कुतः ।
अज्ञानिजनबोधार्थं प्रारब्धं वक्ति वै श्रुतिः ॥

अपरोक्षानुभूतिः.

† सर्वमेवेह हि सदा संसारे रघुनन्दन ।
सम्यक् प्रयुक्तात्सर्वेण पौरुषात्समवाप्यते ॥

योगवासिष्ठम्.

‡ अपि पौरुषमादेयं शास्त्रं चेद्युक्तिबोधकम् ।
अन्यत्त्वार्षमपि त्याज्यं भाव्यं न्याय्यैकसेविना ॥

योगवासिष्ठम्.

CCCV.

THE wise, relying on necessity, should not give up free personal effort, for even necessity works through freedom.*

Yogavâsishtha.

CCCVI.

HE who sets himself not at liberty by cutting up the tight bond—his mind—with his mind, can never be freed by any one else.†

Yogavâsishtha.

ix.—Jna'na (gnosis).

CCCVII.

GNOSIS is, of all means, the only direct means of liberation; liberation is never accomplished without *gnosis* as sure as food is not cooked without fire.‡

Âtmabodha.

---

* पौरुषं न परित्याज्यमेतामाश्रित्य धीमता ।
पौरुषेणैव रूपेण नियतिर्हि नियामिका ॥

योगवासिष्ठम्.

† मनसैव मनश्छित्वा पाशं परमबन्धनम् ।
उन्मोचितो न येनात्मा नासावन्येन मोक्ष्यते ॥

योगवासिष्ठम्.

‡ बोधोऽन्यसाधनेभ्यो हि साक्षान्मोक्षैकसाधनम् ।
पाकस्य वन्हिवज्ज्ञानं विना मोक्षो न सिध्यति ॥

आत्मबोधः.

CCCVIII.

THE fact of the matter is seen by *reflection* engendered through some beneficent suggestion; it can never be seen by constant washing, by giving gifts, nay not even by a hundred *Prâṇâyâmas*.*

Vivekachudâmaṇi.

CCCIX.

THE state of *Brahman* is within reach of those alone who are full of austerity, matrimonial virtue, and truthfulness. Those, indeed, find that entirely pure condition, in whom there is not the remotest trace of fashionable lies or deliberate falsehoods, nor any hypocrisy whatever.†

Praśnopanishad.

CCCX—CCCXI.

WHEN entirely disappear all desires rankling in the heart, the mortal becomes immortal, and fully realizes *Brahman* even here. When here, indeed, burst all ties that

---

* अर्थस्य निश्चयो दृष्टो विचारेण हितोक्तितः ।
न स्नानेन न दानेन प्राणायामशतेन वा ॥

विवेकचूडामणि.

† तेषामेवैष ब्रह्मलोको येषां तपो ब्रह्मचर्यं येषु सत्यं प्रतिष्ठितम् ।
तेषामसौ विरजोब्रह्मलोको न येषु जिम्हमनृतं न माया चेति ॥

प्रश्नोपनिषत्.

bind the heart so fast, the mortal does no doubt become immortal. This verily is the teaching (of the whole of the *Vedânta*).*

Kathopanishad.

CCCXII.

NO means other than *reflection* can produce (real) *gnosis*; nothing but light can ever reveal the existence of things.†

Aparokshânubhuti.

CCCXIII—CCCXV.

REFLECTION may run as follow:—Who am I? How is this evolved? Who can be the creator of this? What may be the material cause? And it may proceed to answer the questions thus:—I am not the body—a mere cluster of elements,—nor even the senses; but I am something quite different from

---

* यदा सर्वे प्रमुच्यन्ते कामा येऽस्य हृदि श्रिताः।
अथ मर्त्योऽमृतो भवत्यत्र ब्रह्म समश्नुते ॥
यदा सर्वे प्रभिद्यन्ते हृदयस्येह ग्रन्थयः।
अथ मर्त्योऽमृतो भवत्येतावदनुशासनम् ॥

कठोपनिषत्.

† नोत्पद्यते विना ज्ञानं विचारेणान्यसाधनैः।
यथा पदार्थभानं हि प्रकाशेन विना क्वचित् ॥

अपरोक्षानुभूतिः.

the one as well as the other. Things come out of ignorance, die away on the rise of *gnosis*, the variety of ideas is the creator.*

Aparokshânubhuti.

CCCXVI.

REFLECTION must be supposed to have borne fruit in that man of good intellect, who continues to lose, from day to day, all avidity for enjoyment.†

Yogavâsishtha.

CCCXVII.

DEPTH such as of the ocean; firmness such as of the Meru; and internal coolness such as of the moon;—these arise in the man devoted to *reflection*.‡

Yogavâsishtha.

---

* कोऽहं कथमिदं जातं को वै कर्त्तास्य विद्यते ।
उपादानं किमस्तीह विचारः सोऽयमीदृशः ॥
नाहं भूतगणो देहो नाहं चाक्षगणस्तथा ।
एतद्विलक्षणः कश्चिद्विचारः सोऽयमीदृशः ॥
अज्ञानप्रभवं सर्वं ज्ञानेन प्रविलीयते ।
संकल्पो विविधः कर्त्ता विचारः सोऽयमीदृशः ॥

अपरोक्षानुभूतिः.

† विचारः सफलस्तस्य विज्ञेयो यस्य सन्मतेः ।
दिनानुदिनमायाति तानवं भोगगृध्नुता ॥

योगवासिष्ठम.

‡ समुद्रस्येवगाम्भीर्यं धैर्यं मेरोरिव स्थितम् ।
अन्तः शीतलता चेन्दोरिवोदेति विचारिणः ॥

योगवासिष्ठम्.

x.—The Sa'dhanas.

CCCXVIII.

THE *four* means (of Self-realization) beginning with non-attachment, come about from keeping all forms prescribed for the class (*varṇa*) one belongs to, by austerity, and by satisfiying Hari with devotion.*

Aparokshânubhuti.

CCCXIX.

CONTROL, give, sympathise; these three must be learnt and practised: Self-control, charity, and sympathy.†

Bṛhadâraṇyakopanishad.

CCCXX.

THOU hankerest after unrealities such as 'I' and 'mine,' those who *know* wish thy activity were directed to the highest reality. *Thou* never canst know the thing nor can *I*. It is meet, therefore, oh mind! for thee to turn to self-restraint.‡

Upadesasâhasri.

---

* स्ववर्णाश्रमधर्मेण तपसा हरितोषणात् ।
साधनं प्रभवेत्पुंसां वैराग्यादिचतुष्टयम् ॥

अपरोक्षानुभूतिः.

† दाम्यत दत्त दयध्वमिति तदेतत्त्रयं शिक्षेद्दमन्दानन्दयामिति ।

बृहदारण्यकोपनिषत्.

‡ अहं ममेति त्वमनर्थमीहसे परार्थमिच्छन्ति तवान्य ईहितम् ।
न तेऽर्थबोधो न हि मेऽस्ति चार्थिता ततश्च युक्तः शम एव ते मनः ॥

उपदेशसाहस्री.

CCCXXI—CCCXXIV.

SELF-restraint consists in freedom from latent desire; and Control, in checking the activity of the external senses. That is the height of Non-attachment which turns the mind entirely away from the objective; that is the best of Indifference which patiently puts up with all evils whatever. Faith is full confidence in sacred texts and their interpreters; and constant oneness of aim in the mind's fixing on the eternal *sat*, is called Pacification (of the mind). Oh my fate! when and how shall I get rid of the bonds of this world—this firm and burning desire may be described as the Desire-for-Liberation.*

Aparokshânubhuti.

CCCXXV.

WHERE these—Non-attachment and Desire-for-liberation—are as yet in the initial stage, there can but appear a mere glimpse of Self-restraint and the rest, even like a glimpse of water in the mirage.†

Vivekachudâmaṇi.

* सदैव वासनात्यागः शमोऽयमिति शब्दितः ।
निग्रहो बाह्यवृत्तीनां दम इत्यभिधीयते ॥
विषयेभ्यः परावृत्तिः परमोपरतिर्हि सा ।
सहनं सर्वदुःखानां तितिक्षा सा शुभा मता ॥
निगमाचार्यवाक्येषु भक्तिः श्रद्धेति विश्रुता ।
चित्तैकाग्र्यं तु सल्लक्ष्ये समाधानमिति स्मृतम् ॥
संसारबन्धनिर्मुक्तिः कथं मे स्यात्कदा विधे ।
इति या सुदृढा बुद्धिर्वक्तव्या सा मुमुक्षुता ॥

अपरोक्षानुभूतिः.

† एतयोर्मन्दता यत्र विरक्तत्वमुमुक्षयोः ।
मरौ सलिलवत् तत्र शमादेर्भानमात्रता ॥

विवेकचूडामणिः.

CCCXXVI.

THE deer, the elephant, the moth, the fish, the bee ;—each of these five is led to destruction by (too much indulgence in each of the five objects of the) five (senses, respectively). How then is it possible that he should escape who lets loose all his five senses in all these five objects, and is never on the alert, besides.*

Bhâgavata.

CCCXXVII.

OH Bhârata ! all beings whatever lose themselves in the world through that illusion, oh destroyer of enemies ! which lies in the very nature of the pairs of opposites (making up the world) and which is born of likes and dislikes (inseparably bound up with those pairs).†

Bhagavadgitâ.

---

* कुरङ्गमातङ्गपतङ्गमीन-
भृङ्गा हताः पञ्चभिरेव पञ्च ।
एकः प्रमादी स कथं न हन्यते
यः सेवते पञ्चभिरेव पञ्च ॥

भागवतम्.

† इच्छाद्वेषसमुत्थेन द्वन्द्वमोहेन भारत ।
सर्वभूतानि सम्मोहं सर्गे यान्ति परन्तप ॥

भगवद्गीता.

CCCXXVIII.

THE wild mare—hope—breaking away to the longest distance, and running back as often, keeps roving about up to the very ends of the quarters.*

Yogavâsishtha.

CCCXXIX.

HE alone *sees* who looks upon another's wife as upon his own mother, who looks upon another's wealth as upon so much earth and stone, who looks upon every being as upon his own Self.†

Smṛti.

CCCXXX—CCCXXXI.

TO the fishes—these men— in the pond of birth and death, wallowing in the slough of the mind, bad latent desires serve for the line to which the woman stands attached as the treacherous bait. He feels desire for enjoyment who has

---

* दूरं दूरमितो गत्वा समेत्य च पुनःपुनः ।
भ्रमत्याशु दिगन्तेषु तृष्णोन्मत्ता तुरङ्गमी ॥

योगवासिष्ठम्.

† मातृवत्परदारेषु परद्रव्येषु लोष्ठवत् ।
आत्मवत्सर्वभूतेषु यः पश्यति स पश्यति ॥

स्मृतिः.

woman (about him); there can be no place for enjoyment to the womanless. Abandon woman, and you abandon the whole world; abandoning the whole world, you find supreme happiness.*

Yogavâsishtha.

CCCXXXII.

NEVER share the same bed or seat even with mother, sister, or daughter; the host of the senses is overwhelmingly powerful, it overpowers even the wise.†

Smṛti.

CCCXXXIII.—CCCXXXIV.

WEALTH, ever on the move, clouds the intellect, nips the line of virtues in the very bud, and betrays into the net

---

* जन्मपल्वलमत्स्यानां चित्तकर्दमचारिणाम् ।
पुंसां दुर्वासनारज्जुर्नारी बडिशपिण्डिका ॥
यस्य स्त्री तस्य भोगेच्छा निःस्त्रीकस्य क्व भोगभूः ।
स्त्रियं त्यक्त्वा जगत्त्यक्तं जगत्त्यक्त्वा सुखी भवेत् ॥

योगवासिष्ठम्.

† मात्रा स्वस्रा दुहित्रा वा नैकशय्यासनो भवेत् ।
बलवानिन्द्रियग्रामो विद्वांसमपि कर्षति ॥

स्मृतिः.

of misery. The man is warm and soft and all that is desirable, to his own and to the world, only as long as he is not sufficiently hardened by wealth, like water by the cold blast.*

Yogavâsishtha.

CCCXXXV.

MISERY attends the acquisition of wealth, and misery attends the protection of wealth acquired; there is misery in its coming, there is misery in its going;—oh! fie upon wealth, the abode of misery out and out.†

Panchatantra.

CCCXXXVI.

THERE is no hope of immortality through wealth (and all it may accomplish of good or religion.)‡

Bṛhadâraṇyakopanishad.

---

* मोहयन्ति मनोवृत्तिं खण्डयन्ति गुणावलिम् ।
दुःखजालं प्रयच्छन्ति विप्रलम्भपराः श्रियः ॥
तावच्छीतमृदुस्पर्शः परे स्वे च जने जनः ।
वात्ययेव हिमं यावच्छ्रिया न परुषीकृतः ॥

योगवासिष्ठम्.

† अर्थानामर्जने दुःखमर्जितानां च रक्षणे ।
आये दुःखं व्यये दुःखं धिगर्थान् कष्टसंश्रयान् ॥

पञ्चतन्त्रम्.

‡ अमृतत्वस्य तु नाशास्ति वित्तेनेति ॥

बृहदारण्यकोपनिषत्.

CCCXXXVII.

ALL growing ends in fading, all rising ends in falling, all meeting ends in parting;—such indeed is the law of this world.*

Yogavâsishtha.

CCCXXXVIII.

OH Yâjnavalkya! what would your worship mean by the All? which is beyond hunger and thirst, beyond sorrow and illusion, beyond decay and death? It is this *âtman* knowing which, *Brâhmaṇas*, ṛenouncing all contact with world, wealth and wife, go about as religious mendicants.†

Bṛhadâraṇyakopanishad.

CCCXXXIX.

OBJECTS of desire, even though they should abide long, are sure to depart. What difference does it make in the *parting* that men do not part from them of their own accord?

---

* सर्वे क्षयान्ता निचयाः प्रलयान्ताः समुच्छ्रयाः ।
संयोगा विप्रयोगान्ताः सर्वे संसारवर्त्मनि ॥

योगवासिष्ठम्.

† कतमो याज्ञवल्क्य सर्वान्तरो योऽशनायापिपासे शोकं मोहं जरां मृत्युमत्येत्येतं वैतमात्मानं विदित्वा ब्राह्मणाः पुत्रैषणायाश्च वित्तैषणायाश्च लोकैषणायाश्च व्युत्थायाथ भिक्षाचर्यं चरन्ति ॥

बृहदारण्यकोपनिषत्.

If they depart of themselves, they leave immeasurable mental suffering behind, if you part from them they confer on you the endless bliss of self-restraint.*

Vairâgyaśataka.

CCCXL.

DEATH is the law of being; the wise describe the exception as 'life'.†

Miscellaneous.

CCCXLI.

THOU grievest where there is nothing to grieve, and thus deludest thyself in parroting the words of the wise:—the wise do verily never grieve either for the dead or for the living.‡

Bhagavadgitâ.

---

* अवश्यं यातारश्चिरतरमुषित्वापि विषया
वियोगे को भेदस्त्यजति न जनो यत्स्वयममून् ।
व्रजन्तः स्वातन्त्र्यादतुलपरितापाय मनसः
स्वयं त्यक्ता ह्येते शमसुखमनन्तं विदधति ॥

भर्तृहरिः.

† मरणं प्रकृतिः शरीरिणां ।
विकृतिर्जीवितमुच्यते बुधैः ॥

प्रास्ताविकः

‡ अशोच्यानन्वशोचस्त्वं प्रज्ञावादांश्च भाषसे ।
गतासूनगतासूंश्च नानुशोचन्ति पण्डिताः ॥

भगवद्गीता.

CCCXLII.

AS the embodied soul passes even in this same body from childhood to youth and age, so does he pass on from one body to another ;—the enlightened finds no cause for grief in the process.*

Bhagavadgitâ.

CCCXLIII.

TO the really enlightened, this great city—his body—is, like a garden, opening up a passage to liberation through enjoyment, thus all bliss and no pain whatever.†

Yogavâsishtha.

CCCXLIV.

OH Bhârata ! beings come out of the unmanifest, and return into the unmanifest; *existing* only in the interval;—where is there any room for grief ?‡

Bhagavadgitâ.

---

* देहिनोऽस्मिन्यथा देहे कौमारं यौवनं जरा ।
तथा देहान्तरप्राप्तिर्धीरस्तत्र न मुह्यति ॥

भगवद्गीता.

† तस्येयं भोगमोक्षार्थं तज्ज्ञस्योपवनोपमा ।
सुखायैव न दुःखाय स्वशरीरमहापुरी ॥

योगवासिष्ठम्.

‡ अव्यक्तादीनि भूतानि व्यक्तमध्यानि भारत ।
अव्यक्तनिधनान्येव तत्र का परिदेवना ॥

भगवद्गीता.

CCCXLV.

THE mind only half informed, and not yet in full realization of the spotless condition, feels the keenest torture in tearing itself away from objects of enjoyment.*

Yogavâsishtha.

CCCXLVI.

WITH every connection the poor thing binds nearer itself, is driven an additional spike into its heart of heart.†

Mahâbhârata.

CCCXLVII—CCCXLVIII.

FROM man's contemplating upon objects comes about attachment to them leading to desire for their acquisition. Desire leads to anger which, through the temporary madness it creates, leads to loss of the memory (of Self). Loss of memory leads to obscuration of the light of spirit; and this darkness is the way to certain ruin.‡

Bhagavadgitâ.

---

* अर्धप्राप्तविवेकस्य न प्राप्तस्यामलं पदम् ।
चेतसस्त्यजतो भोगान् परितापो भृशं भवेत् ॥

योगवासिष्ठम्.

† यावन्तः कुरुते जन्तुः सम्बन्धान् मनसः प्रियान् ।
तावन्तोऽस्य निखन्यन्ते हृदये शोकशङ्कवः ॥

महाभारतम्.

‡ ध्यायतो विषयान्पुंसः सङ्गस्तेषूपजायते ।
सङ्गात्सञ्जायते कामः कामात्क्रोधोऽभिजायते ॥
क्रोधाद्भवति सम्मोहः सम्मोहात्स्मृतिविभ्रमः ।
स्मृतिभ्रंशाद्बुद्धिनाशो बुद्धिनाशात्प्रणश्यति ॥

भगवद्गीता.

CCCXLIX—CCCLI.

FULL of the waters of mental creations, boisterous with the waves of latent desire, infested with the crocodile of attachment, the resort of the birds of imagination, carrying along its mad stream the trees of fortitude growing upon its bank, difficult to cross on account of the treacherous eddies of illusion, enclosed within the impassably high banks of anxiety ;—thus supremely terrible runs the river of Hope. The lords of ascetics, with their minds purified of all dross, rejoice in eternal joy, having crossed over to the other side.*

Vairâgyaśataka.

THERE is the greatest misery in hope, in hopelessness is the height of bliss.†

EVERYTHING that depends on Self is bliss, everything that depends on another is misery.‡

Manu.

CCCLII.

A mere cover of bark satisfies us, you seek satisfaction in wealth and luxury; the feeling, however, is the same

---

* आशा नाम नदी मनोरथजला तृष्णातरङ्गाकुला
रागग्राहवती वितर्कविहगा धैर्यद्रुमध्वंसिनी ।
मोहावर्तसुदुस्तरातिगहना प्रोत्तुङ्गचिन्तातटी
तस्याः पारगता विशुद्धमनसो नन्दन्तु योगीश्वराः ॥

भर्तृहरिः.

† आशायां परमं दुःखं नैराश्यं परमं सुखम् ।

---

‡ सर्वं परवशं दुःखं सर्वमात्मवशं सुखम् ॥

मनुः.

in either case, and the difference is really no difference at all. He, indeed, is the miserable man of poverty who has in him the most insatiable desire; the mind being all contentment what can make the rich or the poor ?*

Vairâgyaśataka.

CCCLIII.

OH my heart ! to secure what favour dost thou enter this slough of worry and distraction in trying to please the mind of others ? If thou wouldst only please thyself, there would, indeed, dawn of itself, on thee, the power of that jewel which is known to fulfil every desire;—what wish, then, of thine will remain unfulfilled, on the merest thought of the moment †?

Vairâgyaśataka.

CCCLIV.

WHAT can be said to the man who finds fault even with him who values at its proper worth all rubbish and its belongings!‡

Nâishkarmyasiddhi.

---

* वयमिह परितुष्टा वल्कलैस्त्वं च लक्ष्म्या
सम इह परितोषो निर्विशेषो विशेषः ।
स तु भवतु दरिद्रो यस्य तृष्णा विशाला
मनसि च परितुष्टे कोऽर्थवान् को दरिद्रः ॥

भर्तृहरिः.

† परेषां चेतांसि प्रतिदिवसमाराध्य बहु हा
प्रसादं किं नेतुं विशसि हृदय क्लेशकलिलम् ।
प्रसन्ने त्वय्यन्तः स्वयमुदितचिन्तामणिगुणे
विमुक्तः संकल्पः किमभिलषितं पुष्यति न ते ॥

भर्तृहरिः.

‡ सपरिकरे वर्चस्के दोषतश्चावधारिते ।
यदि दोषं वदेत्तस्मै किं तत्रोच्चरितुर्भवेत् ॥

नैष्कर्म्यसिद्धिः.

CCCLV.

THERE is no remedy, within knowledge, which can satisfy each and all. Attend, every way, to thy own good, what can the many-tongued world do to thee ?*

In the Jivanmuktiviveka.

CCCLVI—CCCLVII.

WHEN men desirous of doing good, give up even wealth acquired with considerable pains, for the pleasure of others, I would consider it an unmixed good, brought about without any trouble, if men should find satisfaction in speaking ill of me. In this world where we stumble upon poverty of spirit at every step, and which is devoid of every kind of happiness, if any being should find pleasure in speaking ill of me, let him by all means indulge in his feeling, either in my presence or behind my back, for, in this world, all misery, it is very hard to come across even a single moment of such pleasure.†

Jnânânkuśa.

---

* विद्यते न खलु कश्चिदुपायः सर्वलोकपरितोषकरो यः ।
सर्वथा स्वहितमाचरणीयं किं करिष्यति जनो बहुजल्पः ॥

जीवन्मुक्तिविवेके.

† मन्निन्दया यदि जनः परितोषमेति
नन्वप्रयत्नजनितोऽयमनुग्रहो मे ।
श्रेयोऽर्थिनो हि पुरुषाः परतुष्टिहेतो-
र्दुःखार्जितान्यपि धनानि परित्यजन्ति ॥
सततसुलभदैन्ये निःसुखे जीवलोके
यदि मम परिवादात्प्रीतिमाप्नोति कश्चित् ।
परिवदतु यथेष्टं मत्समक्षं तिरो वा
जगति हि बहुदुःखे दुर्लभः प्रीतियोगः ॥

ज्ञानाङ्कुशः.

CCCLVIII.

If the wise man of the world who carefully picks holes in the character of others, expends the same skill on himself, what would prevent him from breaking through the bonds (of ignorance).*

Smṛti.

CCCLIX.

If thou feelest anger at him who does by thee the smallest evil, why dost thou not feel anger at the passion itself which entirely spoils all the four chief aims of existence:—Religion, Property, Enjoyment, Liberation.†

In the Jivanmuktiviveka.

CCCLX.

He who, full of discrimination, sees one equal Self in friends and foes as well as in himself, can feel as much angry with any one, as he should with a part of himself.‡

The Vârtika.

---

* यथा सुनिपुणः सम्यक्परदोषेक्षणेरतः ।
तथा चेन्निपुणः स्वेषु को न मुच्येत बन्धनात् ॥

स्मृतिः,

† अपकारिणि कोपश्चेत्कोपे कोपः कथं न ते ।
धर्मार्थकाममोक्षाणां प्रसह्य परिपन्थिनि ॥

जीवन्मुक्तिविवेके.

‡ रिपौ बन्धौ स्वदेहे च समैकात्म्यं प्रपश्यतः ।
विवेकिनः कुतः कोपः स्वदेहावयवेष्विव ॥

वार्तिकम्

CCCLXI—CCCLXII.

LIFE is as dear to all beings as it is to oneself; feel compassion for every being taking thy own Self as the measure.*

Smṛti.

LET all be happy; let all enjoy perfect health; let all find the good of their heart; let no one come to grief.†

In the Jivanmuktiviveka.

CCCLXIII.

THE triad of the *Veda*, the *Sânkhya*, the *Yoga*, the *Pâsupata*, the *Vaishṇava*;—the three *prasthânas* being interpreted into one or other of these, men look upon this as good and upon that as agreeable, and so on. Of men thus betaking themselves to a variety of ways,—straight, easy or difficult,—on

---

* प्राणा यथात्मनोऽभीष्टा भूतानामपि ते तथा ।
आत्मौपम्येन भूतानां दयां कुर्वीत मानवः ॥

स्मृतिः.

† सर्वेऽत्र सुखिनः सन्तु सर्वे सन्तु निरामयाः ।
सर्वे भद्राणि पश्यन्तु मा कश्चिद्दुःखमाप्नुयात् ॥

जीवन्मुक्तिविवेके.

account of the difference of intellect, Thou alone art the ultimate resort even like the ocean of all water whatever.*

Pushpadantâchârya.

CCCLXIV.

AS the ass carrying a load of sandal-wood is conscious only of the burden, not of the fragrant wood, so, indeed, does he carry them about like a mere burden who having studied the *S'astras* knows not their real import and essence.†

Uttaragitâ.

CCCLXV.

I accept them in the spirit they approach Me, for, oh Arjuna! whatever way men go they follow the path that leads to Me.‡

Bhagavadgitâ.

---

* त्रयी सांख्यं योगः पशुपतिमतं वैष्णवमिति
प्रभिन्ने प्रस्थाने परमिदमदः पथ्यमिति च ।
रुचीनां वैचित्र्यादृजुकुटिलनानापथजुषां
नृणामेको गम्यस्त्वमसि पयसामर्णव इव ॥

पुष्पदन्ताचार्याः.

† यथा खरश्चन्दनभारवाही
भारस्य वेत्ता न तु चन्दनस्य ।
तथैव शास्त्राणि बहून्यधीत्य
सारञ्च जानन्खरवद्वहेत्सः ॥

उत्तरगीता.

‡ ये यथा मां प्रपद्यन्ते तांस्तथैव भजाम्यहम् ॥
मम वर्त्मानुवर्तन्ते मनुष्याः पार्थ सर्वशः ॥

भगवद्गीता.

CCCLXVI.

AS water dropped from the sky seeks the ocean, worship rendered to any deity whatever reaches the lord Keśava.*

Bhâgavata.

CCCLXVII.

THAT which is *not* to be, shall never *be*, that which is to *be* shall never *not* be;—why dost thou not drain this draught which will eradicate the poison of anxiety from thyself?†

Vairâgyaśataka.

CCCLXVIII.

WHAT means the shaft of love? after youth has gone by; what means the lake? after the water is dried up; what means friends and relatives? after all wealth is gone; what means the world? after the Essence is realized.‡

S'ankarâchârya.

---

* आकाशात्पतितं तोयं यथा गच्छति सागरम्।
सर्वदेवनमस्कारः केशवं प्रति गच्छति ॥

भागवतम्.

† यदभावि न तद्भावि भावि चेन्न तदन्यथा।
इति चिन्ताविषघ्नोऽयमगदः किं न पीयते ॥

भर्तृहरिः.

‡ वयसि गते कः कामविकारः
शुष्के नीरे कः कासारः।
क्षीणे वित्ते कः परिवारो
ज्ञाते तत्त्वे कः संसारः ॥

चर्पटपञ्जरिका.

CCCLXIX.

THE ascetic with the matted hair, the mendicant with the shaved head, the *Yati* with the hair rooted out, and many an other of the same class, play a variety of parts, under the cloth dyed yellow-red ;—people though seeing fail thus to see, and go through an amount of trouble for the sake of the belly.*

S'ankarâchârya.

CCCLXX.

DAY follows upon night, evening succeeds morning, the blast of withering cold follows the season full of flowers, and this over and over again ;—time plays with the life of beings thus wearing out; and yet the whirl of hope does never subside.†

S'ankarâchârya.

---

* जटिलो मुण्डी लुञ्चितकेशः
काषायाम्बरबहुधृतवेषः ।
पश्यन्नपि न च पश्यति लोक
उदरनिमित्तं बहुकृतशोकः ॥

चर्पटपञ्जरिका.

† दिनमपि रजनी सायं प्रातः
शिशिरवसन्तौ पुनरायातः ।
कालः क्रीडति गच्छत्यायु-
स्तदपि न मुञ्चत्याशावायुः ॥

चर्पटपञ्जरिका.

CCCLXXI.

ONE beam meets another in the dash of the great ocean, and becomes immediately seperated in the same manner; similar indeed is the meeting of beings with beings.*

Mahâbhârata.

---

xi.—Yoga.

CCCLXXII.

LIBERATION is not on the other side of the sky, nor in the nether world, nor on earth; liberation lies in the mind purified by proper *gnosis.*†

Yogavâsishtha.

CCCLXXIII.

HE alone is fit to inquire after *Brahman*, who has acquired full discrimination, who is firm in non-attachment, who has in him the qualities beginning with self-control, and who, thus qualified, feels keen desire for *knowledge.*‡

Aparokshânubhuti.

---

* यथा काष्ठं च काष्ठं च समेयातां महोदधौ।
समेत्य च व्यपेयातां तद्वद् भूतसमागमः॥

महाभारतम्.

† न मोक्षो नभसः पृष्ठे न पाताले न भूतले।
मोक्षो हि चेतो विमलं सम्यग्ज्ञानविबोधितम्॥

योगवासिष्ठम्.

‡ विवेकिनो विरक्तस्य शमादिगुणशालिनः।
मुमुक्षोरेव हि ब्रह्मजिज्ञासायोग्यता मता॥

अपरोक्षानुभूतिः.

CCCLXXIV.

I have studied enough of philosophy, nay I have talked and taught it to my full; I am convinced there is no condition higher than that silence which comes of the abandonment of all latent desire.*

Yogavâsishtha.

CCCLXXV—CCCLXXVI.

THAT is called the highest condition wherein all the five senses and the mind remain in full control and wherein even the intellect does not pass out to other desires. This steadying of the senses is called *Yoga*; the *Yogin* is full awake in that condition, for, *Yoga* is *creating* accompanied with *giving up*.†

Kathopanishad.

CCCLXXVII.

FIRM and studious application to one essence, suspension of breath, and control of mind;—this is a short statement of the import of 'liberation.'‡

Yogavâsishtha.

---

* विचारितमलं शास्त्रं चिरमुद्ग्राहितं मिथः ।
संत्यक्तवासनान्मौनादृते नास्त्युत्तमं पदम् ॥

योगवासिष्ठम्.

† यदा पञ्चावतिष्ठन्ते ज्ञानानि मनसा सह ।
बुद्धिश्च न विचेष्टेत तामाहुः परमां गतिम् ॥
तां योगमिति मन्यन्ते स्थिरामिन्द्रियधारणाम् ।
अप्रमत्तस्तदा भवति योगो हि प्रभवाप्ययौ ॥

कठोपनिषत्.

‡ एकतत्त्वघनाभ्यासः प्राणानां विलयस्तथा ।
मनोविनिग्रहश्चेति मोक्षशब्दार्थसङ्ग्रहः ॥

योगवासिष्ठम्.

CCCLXXVIII.

TWO, oh Raghava! are the paths leading to suspension of *thinking: Yoga* which consists in controlling transformation of the thinking principle, and *gnosis* which consists in the *proper* eye for experience.*

Yogavâsishtha.

CCCLXXIX.

YOGA is the preventing the transformation of the thinking principle.†

Patanjali.

CCCLXXX.

THE thing to be known can never be known till it is not apprehended by applying Self to Self, of once's own Self, through *reflection*.‡

Yogavâsishtha.

CCCLXXXI.

CONTROL of speech, full independence, absence of hope and desire, and constant love of seclusion,—these open the first door to *Yoga*.§

Vivekachudâmaṇi.

---

* द्वौ क्रमौ चित्तनाशस्य योगो ज्ञानं च राघव ।
योगस्तद्वृत्तिरोधो हि ज्ञानं सम्यगवेक्षणम् ॥

योगवासिष्ठम्.

† योगश्चित्तवृत्तिनिरोधः ॥

पातञ्जलसूत्रम्.

‡ स्वयमेव विचारेण विचार्यात्मानमात्मना ।
यावन्नाधिगतं ज्ञेयं न तावदधिगम्यते ॥

योगवासिष्ठम्.

§ योगस्य प्रथमद्वारं वाङ्निरोधोऽपरिग्रहः ।
निराशा च निरीहा च नित्यमेकान्तशीलता ॥

विवेकचूडामणिः.

CCCLXXXII—CCCLXXXIV.

IT (the mind) is controlled by practice and non-attachment.*

Patanjali.

Experience ceases not even in the absence of objects, to him who always thinks of them, even like the experience which, as it were, comes out of nothing in dream.—Lead, therefore, the mind addicted to the ways of vice, to obey control, by means such as unqualified devotion and non-attachment.†

Bhâgavata.

CCCLXXXV.

GNOSIS, dissolution of mind, and destruction of latent desire, these being the reciprocal causes, one of the other, are most difficult to accomplish.‡

Yogavâsishtha.

---

* अभ्यासवैराग्याभ्यां तन्निरोधः ॥

पातञ्जलसूत्रम्.

† अर्थे ह्यविद्यमानेऽपि संसृतिर्न निवर्तते ।
ध्यायतो विषयानस्य स्वप्नेऽनर्थागमो यथा ॥
अत एव शनैश्चित्तं प्रसक्तमसतां पथि ।
भक्तियोगेन तीव्रेण विरक्त्या च नयेद्वशम् ॥

भागवतम्.

‡ तत्त्वज्ञानं मनोनाशो वासनाक्षय एव च ।
मिथः कारणतां गत्वा दुःसाध्यानि स्थितान्यतः ॥

योगवासिष्ठम्.

CCCLXXXVI—CCCLXXXVII.

YOGA is not possible in him who eats much, nor is it possible in him who eats too little. It is not possible in him who likes to spend all his time in sleep, nor in him, oh Arjuna! who forces himself to be awake all the while. *Yoga* conduces to the destruction of misery in him who with moderate nourishment, moderate enjoyment, and moderate attention to business, takes moderate rest, and keeps himself moderately awake.*

Bhagavadgitâ.

CCCLXXXVIII.

MIND being nearest mind, those who abandoning the true secret, apply themselves only to the body, are described as (lost) in *physical Yoga*.†

Yogavâsishtha.

CCCLXXXIX—CCCXCI.

EVER free from the intellectual 'doubt'; exercising perfect control over the mind through inexhaustible patience; giving up all concern with objects of sense beginning with (pleasant) sounds and the like; free from love and hate; fond of solitude; taking light nourishment; keeping

---

* नात्यश्नतस्तु योगोऽस्ति न चैकान्तमनश्नतः ।
न चातिस्वप्नशीलस्य जाग्रतो नैव चार्जुन ॥
युक्ताहारविहारस्य युक्तचेष्टस्य कर्मसु ।
युक्तस्वप्नावबोधस्य योगो भवति दुःखहा ॥

भगवद्गीता.

† चित्तं चित्तस्य वा दूरे संस्थितं स्वशरीरकम् ।
साधयन्ति समुत्सृज्य युक्तिं ये तान् हठान्विदुः ॥

योगवासिष्ठम्.

tongue, body and mind within proper check ; ever devoted to *Yoga* and deep concentration; firmly fixed in the sense of non-attachment ; rising above egoism, obstinate intolerance, vanity, desire, anger, and love of goods ; ever without self-assertion ;—such a one is fit to *become Brahman.**

Bhagavadgitâ.

CCCXCII.

WHATEVER comes to view in this world, whatever raises you to the sky, whatever exhalts you to heaven ;—everything, oh Rama! is within reach after complete destruction of all love and all hate.†

Yogavâsishtha.

CCCXCIII.

THE *Yogin* striving with unremitting effort, and being completely purified of all dross whatever, is ripened into the supreme condition, passing from stage to stage, through numerous incarnations.‡

Bhagavadgitâ.

---

* बुद्ध्या विशुद्धया युक्तो धृत्यात्मानं नियम्य च ।
शब्दादीन्विषयांस्त्यक्त्वा रागद्वेषौ व्युदस्य च ॥
विविक्तसेवी लघ्वाशी यतवाक्कायमानसः ।
ध्यानयोगपरो नित्यं वैराग्यं समुपाश्रितः ॥
अहङ्कारं बलं दर्पं कामं क्रोधं परिग्रहम् ।
विमुच्य निर्ममः शान्तो ब्रह्मभूयाय कल्पते ॥

भगवद्गीता.

† यत्किञ्चिदुदितं लोके यन्नभस्यथवा दिवि ।
तत्सर्वं प्राप्यते राम रागद्वेषपरिक्षयात् ॥

योगवासिष्ठम्.

‡ प्रयत्नाद्यतमानस्तु योगी संशुद्धकिल्बिषः ।
अनेकजन्मसंसिद्धस्ततो याति परां गतिम् ॥

भगवद्गीता.

CCCXCIV.

HE who is full of *Yoga*, completely purified of all dross, all self-control, ever master of his senses, and above all one with the Self of all and every being, is never affected in the *acting*.*

Bhagavadgitâ.

CCCXCV.

RENOUNCE all concern with the results of *action*, and through this *Yoga* find the peace of self-realization ; ignorance of this *Yoga* leads to bondage through attachment to results, from desires within.†

Bhagavadgitâ.

CCCXCVI.

PRODUCING Self from Self, and, as often, deluding Self by Self, inner conciousness leads itself, of itself, to the bliss of self-realization.‡

Yogavâsishtha.

---

* योगयुक्तो विशुद्धात्मा विजितात्मा जितेन्द्रियः ।
सर्वभूतात्मभूतात्मा कुर्वन्नपि न लिप्यते ॥

भगवद्गीता.

† युक्तः कर्मफलं त्यक्त्वा शान्तिमाप्नोति नैष्ठिकीम् ।
अयुक्तः कामकारेण फले सक्तो निबद्ध्यते ॥

भगवद्गीता.

‡ जनयित्वात्मनात्मानं मोहयित्वा पुनः पुनः ।
स्वयं मोक्षं नयत्यन्तःसंवित्स्वं विद्धि राघव ॥

योगवासिष्ठम्.

CCCXCVII.

ACTIONS do not put him in bondage who, oh, Dhananjaya! has renounced all acts through *Yoga*, and who being cured of (the intellectual) doubt, through proper *gnosis*, has *re*-gained his Self.*

Bhagavadgitá.

CCCXCVIII.

NONE who has not renounced the mental world, has any title to the name '*Yogin.*'†

Bhagavadgitá.

CCCXCIX.

(IF *Yoga* consists in restraining the vital breath) this could easily be done through non-attachment, through constant application to the Cause, through some well-conceived device, through the abandonment of evil habits, or through realization of the Absolute.‡

Yogavásishtha.

---

* योगसंन्यस्तकर्माणं ज्ञानसंछिन्नसंशयम् ।
आत्मवन्तं न कर्माणि निबध्नन्ति धनंजय ॥

भगवद्गीता.

† न ह्यसंन्यस्तसङ्कल्पो योगी भवति कश्चन ॥

भगवद्गीता.

‡ वैराग्यात्कारणाभ्यासाद्युक्तितो व्यसनक्षयात् ।
परमार्थावबोधाच्च रोध्यन्ते प्राणवायवः ॥

योगवासिष्ठम्.

CD.

WE are put in mind of the flame of a lamp protected in some place not open to the breeze, and therefore not flickering any way. The well-controlled mind of the *Yogin* applying himself to the *Yoga* of Self is verily in that condition.*

Bhagavadgitâ.

CDI—CDII.

WHO, deep immersed in the idea of Oneness, devotes himself to Me, present in all beings, is the *yogin* ever *in* Me, though appearing everywhere and anywhere. Oh Arjuna! he is the greatest *yogin* who looks with equal eye upon pleasure or pain, always taking his own Self as the measure.†

Bhagavadgitâ.

CDIII.

DETACH thyself from the thing tasted and from that which tastes it, meditate on the *taste alone;* thus *be* ever all *Âtman.*‡

Yogavâsishtha.

---

* यथा दीपो निवातस्थो नेङ्गते सोपमा स्मृता ।
योगिनो यतचित्तस्य युञ्जतो योगमात्मनः ॥

भगवद्गीता.

† सर्वभूतस्थितं यो मां भजत्येकत्वमास्थितः ।
सर्वथा वर्तमानोऽपि स योगी मयि वर्तते ॥
आत्मौपम्येन सर्वत्र समं पश्यति योऽर्जुन ।
सुखं वा यदि वा दुःखं स योगी परमो मतः ॥

भगवद्गीता.

‡ स्वाद्यस्वादकसन्त्यक्तं स्वाद्यस्वादकमध्यगम् ।
स्वादनं केवलं ध्यायन्नित्यमात्ममयो भव ॥

योगवासिष्ठम्.

CDIV.

WHO attends to all acts whatever which fall to his lot, without attaching himself to the result, is the real *Sannyâsin*, the real *Yogin*, not he who gives up the worship of household-fire,* nor he who suspends all action.†

Bhagavadgitâ.

CDV.

IT is impossible for any embodied being to get rid of action in its entirety; he has best *renounced* action who attaches himself not to the result.‡

Bhagavadgitâ.

CDVI.

THE mind being full, the whole universe is filled with the juice of nectar; the whole earth is covered with leather to him who has put his foot in the shoe.§

Yogavâsishtha.

---

* For, formal religion requires that one going into *Sannyâsa* (renunciation) must give up all concern with the world and therefore with all worship, chiefly worship of that fire which is kept in the house since marriage.

† अनाश्रितः कर्मफलं कार्यं कर्म करोति यः ।
स संन्यासी च योगी च न निरग्निर्न चाक्रियः ॥

भगवद्गीता.

‡ न हि देहभृता शक्यं त्यक्तुं कर्माण्यशेषतः ।
यस्तु कर्मफलत्यागी स त्यागीत्यभिधीयते ॥

भगवद्गीता.

§ पूर्णे मनसि सम्पूर्णं जगत्सर्वं सुधाद्रवैः ।
उपानद्गूढपादस्य ननु चर्मास्तृतेव भूः ॥

योगवासिष्ठम्.

CDVII.

THE wise know that as 'renunciation' (*sannyâsa*) which consists in renunciation of all action coming of *desire*; the informed call that 'abandonment' (*tyâga*) which consists in the abandonment of all concern with the results of action.*

Bhagavadgitâ.

CDVIII.

I think those students will never find their effort end in any good result who without knowing spiritual *yoga* (*Râja-yoga*) address themselves only to physical exercises (*Hatha-yoga*†).‡

Hathapradipika.

CDIX—CDX.

WITH patience and perseverance as its guides, the mind may pacify itself gradually, and by slow degrees. Turn the mind firmly to thy Self, cease to think of anything

---

* काम्यानां कर्मणां न्यासं संन्यासं कवयो विदुः ।
सर्वकर्मफलत्यागं प्राहुस्त्यागं विचक्षणाः ॥

भगवद्गीता.

† *Hatha* is a word peculiarly derived: *Ha*=the breath which flows through the right orifice of the nose; *tha*=the breath which flows the other way. The one is symbolized by the sun, the other by the moon. Hatha-Yoga means the union of the two, the *sushumṇâ*, the time most propitious for concentration.

‡ राजयोगमजानन्तः केवलं हठकर्मिणः ।
एतानभ्यासिनो मन्ये प्रयासफलवर्जितान् ॥

हठप्रदीपिका.

besides; control it back into the Self from wherever this unstable slippery thing should run out of itself.*

Bhagavadgitâ.

CDXI.

DOING and *suffering* being at end, peace alone survives;— this expanded to the absolute limit, the wise call 'liberation.'†

Yogavâsishtha.

CDXII.

TIME must elapse between sowing and harvest, nay even in the growth of such wild grass as the holy *Kuśa* and the like; *reflection* on *Âtman* ripens (into self-realization) by degrees, and in course of time.‡

Panchadaśi.

---

* शनैःशनैरुपरमेद्बुद्ध्या धृतिगृहीतया ।
आत्मसंस्थं मनः कृत्वा न किञ्चिदपि चिन्तयेत् ॥
यतो यतो निश्चरति मनश्चञ्चलमस्थिरम् ।
ततस्ततो नियम्यैतदात्मन्येव वशं नयेत् ॥

भगवद्गीता.

† शान्ते कर्तृत्वभोक्तृत्वे शान्तिरेवेह शिष्यते ।
प्रौढिमभ्यागता सैव मुक्तिरित्युच्यते बुधैः ॥

योगवासिष्ठम्.

‡ कालेन परिपच्यन्ते कृषिदर्भादयो यथा ।
तद्वदात्मविचारोऽपि शनैः कालेन पच्यते ॥

पञ्चदशी.

CDXIII.

ATTACH thyself not to *Karma* ; but equally attach thyself not to stupid inactivity and suspension of all *Karma* whatever ;—*be* what you *are*, equal (in all conditions).*

Yogavâsishtha.

CDXIV.

THAT patience which would empty the ocean drop by drop at the tip of a straw of the *Kuśa*-grass, will, untiringly sustained, establish control over the mind.†

Gaudapâdâchârya.

CDXV.

THE inner Self is the *purusha* as big as the man's thumb ever present in the *heart* ;—him should he patiently separate from the body like its pulp from the straw.‡

Kathopanishad.

---

* कर्मासक्तिमनाश्रित्य तथानाश्रित्य मूढताम् ।
नैष्कर्म्यमप्यनाश्रित्य समस्तिष्ठ यथास्थितम् ॥

योगवासिष्ठम्

† उत्सेक उदधेर्यद्वत्कुशाग्रेणैकबिन्दुना ।
मनसो निग्रहस्तद्वद्भवेदपरिखेदतः ॥

गौडपादाचार्याः.

‡ अङ्गुष्ठमात्रः पुरुषोऽन्तरात्मा सदा जनानां हृदये सन्निविष्टः ।
तं स्वाच्छरीरात्प्रवृहेन्मुञ्जादिवेषीकां धैर्येण ॥

कठोपनिषत्.

CDXVI.

ABANDON all *forms* whatever, betake thyself to Me—the One; I shall point the way out of all misery and sin, never grieve (over thy lot).*

Bhagavadgitâ.

CDXVII—CDXVIII.

THE One, omnipotent, inner Self of all beings, manifests himself as the manifold ;—none but those who see Him in themselves, find eternal happiness. Eternal in the eternal, conscious in the conscious, ever one, he sends out all the variety of ideas to all ;—none but those who see Him in themselves, find eternal peace.†

Kathopanishad.

CDXIX.

THOSE *Yogins* who never suspend effort find It in themselves ; those who have not obtained sight of *Âtman*, and are thus unenlightened, never find It though ever *trying*.‡

Bhagavadgitâ.

---

* सर्वधर्मान्परित्यज्य मामेकं शरणं व्रज ।
अहं त्वा सर्वपापेभ्यो मोक्षयिष्यामि मा शुचः ॥

भगवद्गीता.

† एको वशी सर्वभूतान्तरात्मा एकं रूपं बहुधा यः करोति ।
तमात्मस्थं येऽनुपश्यन्ति धीरास्तेषां सुखं शाश्वतं नेतरेषाम् ॥
नित्यो नित्यानां चेतनश्चेतनानामेको बहूनां यो विदधाति कामान् ।
तमात्मस्थं येऽनुपश्यन्ति धीरास्तेषां शान्तिः शाश्वती नेतरेषाम् ॥

कठोपनिषत्.

‡ यतन्तो योगिनश्चैनं पश्यन्त्यात्मन्यवस्थितम् ।
यतन्तोऽप्यकृतात्मानो नैनं पश्यन्त्यचेतसः ॥

भगवद्गीता.

CDXX.

THE interval between the mind's passing from one idea to another, all blank and free from any thinking whatever, may be described as the native condition (of Self).*

Yogavâsishtha.

CDXXI.

HE finds not peace who runs after objects of desire. He indeed finds peace whose heart with all desires entering into it ever stands like the ocean. All waters flow continually into the ocean, and yet he never transgresses his limit.†

Bhagavadgitâ.

CDXXII.

FIX thy mind on that which is not smitten with the evil eye of the Devil of Multifariousness,—causing shakiness of mind.‡

Yogavâsishtha.

---

* अर्थादर्थान्तरं चित्ते याति मध्ये हि या स्थितिः।
निरस्तमनना यासौ स्वरूपस्थितिरुच्यते ॥

योगवासिष्ठम्.

† आपूर्यमाणमचलप्रतिष्ठं
समुद्रमापः प्रविशन्ति यद्वत् ।
तद्वत् कामा यं प्रविशन्ति सर्वे
स शान्तिमाप्नोति न कामकामी ॥

भगवद्गीता.

‡ यददृष्टमशुद्धेन चित्तवैधुर्यदायिना ।
अनेकत्वपिशाचेन तत्परं कारयेन्मनः ॥

योगवासिष्ठम्.

CDXXIII.

THESE are the three gates to Hell and Self-destruction :— Desire, anger, and greed ; give up these three.*

Bhagavadgitâ.

CDXXIV—CDXXVI.

FEARLESSNESS, purity of heart, steady application to the *yoga* of *gnosis*, charity, self-control, sacrifice, fulfilment of duty, austerity, straight-forwardness, universal love, truthfulness, absence of anger, renunciation, peacefulness, freedom from jealousy, compassion for all beings, firmness of mind, softness of heart, modesty, calmness, agreeable awfulness, forbearance, fortitude, purity, forgiveness, freedom from self-assertion, these, oh Bhârata ! are ever present in him who is born to Life of the Higher Self.†

Bhagavadgitâ.

---

* त्रिविधं नरकस्येदं द्वारं नाशनमात्मनः ।
कामः क्रोधस्तथा लोभस्तस्मादेतत्त्रयं त्यजेत् ॥

भगवद्गीता.

† अभयं सत्वसंशुद्धिर्ज्ञानयोगव्यवस्थितिः ।
दानं दमश्च यज्ञश्च स्वाध्यायस्तप आर्जवम् ॥
अहिंसा सत्यमक्रोधस्त्यागः शान्तिरपैशुनम् ।
दया भूतेष्वलोलुप्त्वं मार्दवं ह्रीरचापलम् ॥
तेजः क्षमा धृतिः शौचमद्रोहो नातिमानिता ।
भवन्ति सम्पदं दैवीमभिजातस्य भारत ॥

भगवद्गीता.

CDXXVII.

HYPOCRISY, impudence, self-assertion, anger, harshness, and ignorance, are seen in those who, oh Son of Pṛthâ ! are born to Life of the Lower Self.*

Bhagavadgitá.

CDXXVIII.

WHAT he *does* and what he *thinks*, that he *becomes*.†

Bṛhadâraṇyakopanishad.

CDXXIX—CDXXXI.

NO being ever lives of *Prâṇa* or *Apâna* ; all beings live of the thing that transcends them, of the thing in which they live. I shall explain to thee, once more, the eternal, esoteric, *Brahman* ; I shall tell thee, oh Gautama ! what becomes of the soul (who knows not *Brahman*) after death. Some of these return into the womb of woman for further incarnation, others assimilate themselves with immovable things,—all in accord with the acts they have done, the Idea they have lived.‡

Kathopanishad.

---

* दम्भो दर्पोऽभिमानश्च क्रोधः पारुष्यमेव च ।
अज्ञानं चाभिजातस्य पार्थ सम्पदमासुरीम् ॥

भगवद्गीता.

† यथाकारी यथाचारी तथा भवति ॥

बृहदारण्यकोपनिषत्.

‡ न प्राणेन नापानेन मर्त्यो जीवति कश्चन ।
इतरेण तु जीवन्ति यस्मिन्नेतावुपाश्रितौ ॥
हन्त त इदम्प्रवक्ष्यामि गुह्यम्ब्रह्मसनातनम् ।
यथा च मरणं प्राप्य आत्मा भवति गौतम ॥
योनिमन्ये प्रपद्यन्ते शरीरत्वाय देहिनः ।
स्थाणुमन्येऽनुसंयन्ति यथाकर्म यथाश्रुतम् ॥

कठोपनिषत्.

CDXXXII.

IN those who do not apply themselves to real *Yoga*, there can be no sense of spiritual culture ; nor firm realization of the Idea. Want of realization of the Idea results in want of peace, and want of peace in want of happiness.*

Bhagavadgitâ.

CDXXXIII—CDXXXIV.

NEITHER speech nor mind, nay not even the eye, can realize It ; how can It be realized in any category other than Being. It should be realized as (pure) Being, through proper analysis of both (its conditioned and unconditioned *forms*) ;—On him breaks the light of the Essence (beyond Being as well as non-Being) who thus realizes It.†

Kathopanishad.

CDXXXV.

SUBJECT is coloured with object, and object is coloured with subject ; both, again, are coloured with the sense of 'egoism,' on the destruction whereof is, therefore, realized the oneness of *Átman*.‡

Naishkarmyasiddhi.

---

* नास्ति बुद्धिरयुक्तस्य न चायुक्तस्य भावना ।
न चाभावयतः शान्तिरशान्तस्य कुतः सुखम् ॥

भगवद्गीता.

† नैव वाचा न मनसा प्राप्तुं शक्यो न चक्षुषा ।
अस्तीति ब्रुवतोऽन्यत्र कथं तदुपलभ्यते ॥
अस्तीत्येवोपलब्धव्यस्तत्त्वभावेन चोभयोः ।
अस्तीत्येवोपलब्धस्य तत्त्वभावः प्रसीदति ॥

कठोपनिषत्.

‡ दृश्यानुरक्तं तद्द्रष्टृ दृश्यं द्रष्ट्रनुरञ्जितम् ।
अहंवृत्त्योभयं रक्तं तन्नाशेऽद्वैततात्मनः ॥

नैष्कर्म्यसिद्धिः.

CDXXXVI.

EGOISM is plainly not destroyed, till all forms and conventions which hold thee fast in bondage, as in a cage, are not annihilated to the extent of leaving absolutely nothing for remainder.*

Yogavâsishtha.

CDXXXVII.

BEING, perception, pleasure, name, and form, these five make up all objects whatever ; the first three make up *Brahman*, the rest this world.†

Dṛgdṛśyaviveka.

CDXXXVIII.

SOME may cognize the ever blissful, the illuminator of all illumination whatever, even by not cognizing It thus.‡

Âtmapurâna.

---

* यन्त्रणापञ्जरं यावद्भग्नं लूनादि नाखिलम् ।
अकिञ्चनत्वशेषेण स्फुटा तावदहङ्कृतिः ॥

योगवासिष्ठम्.

† अस्ति भाति प्रियं रूपं नाम चेत्यंशपञ्चकम् ।
आद्यं त्रयं ब्रह्मरूपं जगद्रूपं ततो द्वयम् ॥

दृग्दृश्यविवेकः.

‡ सदानन्दात्मरूपस्य ज्योतिषां भासकस्य च ।
एवमग्रहणेनैव ग्रहणं कस्यचिद्भवेत् ॥

आत्मपुराणम्.

CDXXXIX.

SAID Yâjnavalkya :—Oh love ! the husband is dear not for himself, but for oneself, the wife is dear not for herself, but for oneself . . . . No one thing is dear for itself, but for ourself ;—this Self should be seen, studied, contemplated, assimilated ; oh sweet Maitreyi ! the study, contemplation, and assimilation of Self leaves nothing to know.*

Bṛhadâraṇyakopanishad.

CDXL—CDXLI.

SAID Yâjnavalkya: It may be seen after the following illustrations : The ocean is the one resort of all water; the skin is the ultimate sphere of all touch ; the tongue is the one ground of all taste; the nose is the one basis of all smell ; the eye is the one field of all form ; the ear is the one place of all sound ; the mind is the one source of all ideas ; the heart is the one fountain of all knowledge ; . . . the Word is the one truth of all the Vedas :—even thus is It the one *fact* of all and every *being*. Put a lump of salt in water, it melts into the water of which it came ; you can never grasp it afterwards ; it is all salt, every drop of water you may touch. So indeed, oh dear one ! is this great, endless unlimited Being,—all thought. (The universe) coming of

---

* स होवाच न वा अरे पत्युः कामाय पतिः प्रियो भवत्यात्मनस्तु कामाय पतिः प्रियो भवति न वा अरे जायायै कामाय जाया प्रिया भवत्यात्मनस्तु कामाय जाया प्रिया भवति।...न वा अरे सर्वस्य कामाय सर्वं प्रियं भवत्यात्मनस्तु कामाय सर्वं प्रियं भवत्यात्मा वारे द्रष्टव्यः श्रोतव्यो मन्तव्यो निदध्यासितव्यो मैत्रेय्यात्मनो वा अरे दर्शनेन श्रवणेन मत्या विज्ञानेनेदं सर्वं विदितम्।

बृहदारण्यकोपनिषत्.

this, melts away into this, and being thus lost, loses all distinction whatever.*

Bṛhadâraṇyakopanishad.

CDXLII—CDXLV.

THE following may serve for fit illustrations:—When a drum is being beaten it is difficult to catch all the noise that proceeds from of it ; the drum itself being seen, the whole of the noise that follows the beating is grasped without mistake. When the conch is being blown it is difficult to mark all the sounds that blow themselves out to all directions; the conch being seen the whole of the sound that blows through it is marked without fail. When the lyer is being played upon, it is difficult to observe the notes passing one into the other ; the lyre being seen, the music flowing through it is seen in a moment. As from fire fed with wet fuel arise sparks and smoke and the like, so is all this, oh dear one! the mere spontaneous breath of the great *Be-ing*: the *Ṛgveda*, the *Yajurveda*, the *Sâmveda*, the *Atharvaveda*, all history, all mythology, all science, all philo-

---

* स यथा सर्वासामपां समुद्र एकायनमेवं सर्वेषां स्पर्शानां त्वगेकायनमेवं सर्वेषां रसानां जिह्वैकायनमेवं सर्वेषां गन्धानां नासिकैकायनमेवं सर्वेषां रूपाणां चक्षुरेकायनमेवं सर्वेषां शब्दानां श्रोत्रमेकायनमेवं सर्वेषां सङ्कल्पानां मन एकायनमेवं सर्वासां विद्यानां हृदयमेकायनं...एवं सर्वेषां वेदानां वागेकायनम् ।

स यथा सैन्धवखिल्य उदके प्रास्त उदकमेवानुविलीयत नाहास्योद्ग्रहणायेव स्याद्यतो यतस्त्वाददीत लवणमेवैवं वा अर इदं महद्भूतमनन्तमपारं विज्ञानघन एवैतेभ्यो भूतेभ्यः समुत्थाय तान्येवानुविनश्यति न प्रेत्य संज्ञास्तीत्यरे ब्रवीमीति होवाच याज्ञवल्क्यः ।

बृहदारण्यकोपनिषत्.

sophy, all poetry, all aphorisms, all commentaries, all parables;—everything is Its breath.*

Bṛhadârṇyakopanishad.

CDXLVI—CDXLVIII.

OH good one! one *form* of clay furnishes the clue to all that is made of clay; all evolutes being mere names, mere play of words; the real ground of them all being all caly and nothing else. One *form* of gold reveals the nature of all forms of the same metal; all evolutes being mere names, mere play of words; the real ground of them all being all gold and nothing else. One *form* of iron leads to all forms whatever of the same metal; all evolutes being mere names, mere play of words; the real ground of them all is all iron and nothing else. Thus oh good one! should be understood what I explained to thee (in the words THOU art THAT).†

Chhândogyopanishad.

---

* स यथा दुन्दुभेर्हन्यमानस्य न बाह्याञ्छब्दाञ्छक्नुयाद्ग्रहणाय दुन्दुभेस्तु ग्रहणेन दुन्दुभ्याघातस्य वा शब्दो गृहीतः ॥

स यथा शङ्खस्य ध्मायमानस्य न बाह्याञ्छब्दाञ्छक्नुयाद्ग्रहणाय शङ्खस्य तु ग्रहणेन शङ्खध्मस्य वा शब्दो गृहीतः ॥

स यथा वीणायै वाद्यमानायै न बाह्याञ्छब्दाञ्छक्नुयाद्ग्रहणाय वीणायै तु ग्रहणेन वीणावादस्य वा शब्दो गृहीतः ॥

स यथार्द्रैधाग्नेरभ्याहितात्पृथग्धूमा विनिश्चरन्त्येवं वा अरेऽस्य महतो भूतस्य निःश्वसितमेतद्यदृग्वेदो यजुर्वेदः सामवेदोऽथर्वाङ्गिरस इतिहासः पुराणं विद्या उपनिषदः श्लोकाः सूत्राण्यनुव्याख्यानानि व्याख्यानान्यस्यैवैतानि सर्वाणि निश्वसितानि ॥

बृहदारण्यकोपानिषत्.

† यथा सौम्यैकेन मृत्पिण्डेन सर्वं मृन्मयं विज्ञातं स्याद्वाचारम्भणं विकारो नामधेयं मृत्तिकेत्येव सत्यम् ॥ १ ॥

यथा सौम्यैकेन लोहमणिना सर्वं लोहमयं विज्ञातं स्याद्वाचारम्भणं विकारो नामधेयं लोहमित्येव सत्यम् ॥ २ ॥

यथा सौम्येकेन नखनिकृन्तनेन सर्वं कार्ष्णायसं विज्ञातं स्याद्वाचारम्भणं विकारो नामधेयं कृष्णायसमित्येव सत्यमेवं सौम्य स आदेशो भवतीति ॥ ३ ॥

छान्दोग्योपनिषत्.

CDXLIX.

EVERY one derives his faith from the inmost tendency of his heart; the man is all faith, he *is* that which he *has* faith in.*

Bhagavadgitâ.

CDL.

WHO thinks *Brahman* is naught becomes naught; he is all being who knows *Brahman* to be.†

Taittiriyopanishad.

CDLI.

THE whole world is *Âtman*, there is no *Avidyâ* anywhere;—betake thyself to this view of things, and rest in peace, thus (re-) gaining thy real self.‡

Yogavâsishtha.

---

* सत्त्वानुरूपा सर्वस्य श्रद्धा भवति भारत ।
श्रद्धामयोऽयं पुरुषो यो यच्छ्रद्धः स एव सः ॥

भगवद्गीता.

† असन्नेव स भवति असद्ब्रह्मेति वेद चेत् ।
अस्ति ब्रह्मेति चेद्वेद सन्तमेनं ततो विदुः ॥

तैत्तिरीयोपनिषत्.

‡ जगदात्मैव सकलमविद्या नास्ति कुत्रचित् ।
इति दृष्टिमवष्टभ्य सम्यग्रूपः स्थिरो भव ॥

योगवासिष्ठम्.

CDLII.

THE man attached to 'being,' is all *being*, through total identification with the Idea; the moth full of the idea of the bee *becomes* the bee*. †

Vivekachudâmaṇi.

CDLIII.

IDENTIFY the mind with that which leads to good in the end, which is all truth, which is everlasting, which is above illusion, and which is not struck with the eye of evil desire.‡

Yogavâsishtha.

CDLIV.

IDENTIFICATION with being leads to *being*, identification with emptiness leads to emptiness, and identification with the All leads to supreme fullness. Study to attain the condition of this fullness.§

Aparokshânubhuti.

---

* The allusion obviously is to the real on supposed habit of yellow bees here. It is said they lay hold of one of the small worms found in putrifying substances an d close it up in their cell. When the cell is opened by the bee after a time, the worm flies out a bee.

† सति सक्तो नरो याति सद्भावं ह्येकनिष्ठया ।
कीटको भ्रमरं ध्यायन् भ्रमरत्वाय कल्पते ॥

विवेकचूडामणिः.

‡ यदुदर्कहितं सत्यमनपायि गतभ्रमम् ।
दुरीहितदृशोन्मुक्तं तत्परं कारयेन्मनः ॥

योगवासिष्ठम्.

§ भाववृत्त्या हि भावत्वं शून्यवृत्त्या हि शून्यता ।
ब्रह्मवृत्त्या हि पूर्णत्वं तथा पूर्णत्वमभ्यसेत् ॥

अपरोक्षानुभूतिः.

CDLV.

THERE is no condition either of bondage or liberation; there is no duality and no unity; it is all being—*Brahman*, out and out. This is the absolute truth.*

Yogavâsishtha.

CDLVI.

THE wise should fuse all speech (and senses) into the mind, the mind into the Self that discriminates (*viz.*, *buddhi*), the discriminating Self into the great Self (*viz.*, the first differentiation in the Self called *mahat*—egoism), and he should fuse this great Self into the Self, all peace and tranquility.†

Kathopanishad.

CDLVII.

HAVING destroyed sense with sense, mind with mind, egoism with egoism, I stand supreme as the *residuum* of all.‡

Yogavâsishtha.

---

* बन्धमोक्षदशाहीना द्वित्वैकत्वविवर्जिता ।
सर्वैव ब्रह्मसत्येयमित्येषा परमार्थता ॥

योगवासिष्ठम्.

† यच्छेद्वाङ्मनसि प्राज्ञस्तद्यच्छेज्ज्ञान आत्मनि ।
ज्ञानमात्मनि महति नियच्छेत्तद्यच्छेच्छान्त आत्मनि ॥

कठोपनिषत्.

‡ इन्द्रियेणेन्द्रियं छित्त्वा छित्त्वा च मनसा मनः ।
अहङ्कृतिमहङ्कृत्या छित्त्वा शेषो जयाम्यहम् ॥

योगवासिष्ठम्.

CDLVIII.

USE for bow the word of glory (*aum*), fix the arrow, thy individual Self, on the string; and being all attention, take such unmissing aim as would dissolve the arrow in the target—*Brahman.**

Muṇdukopanishad.

CDLIX—CDLXI.

TURN the vision inside out by *gnosis* and find the whole world all *Brahman* ; for, this is the true 'fixing of the eye', not that which consists in fixing it on the tip of the nose. The eye should not be directed to the tip of the nose, but to that wherein stands dissolved the triad of subject, object and instrument. True *Prâṇâyâma* (control of breath) consists in that control over the functioning of the mind, which follows upon realization of all objects on the material and mental plane, as *in* and *of Brahman.*†

Aparokshânubhuti.

---

* प्रणवो धनुः शरो ह्यात्मा ब्रह्म तल्लक्ष्यमुच्यते ।
अप्रमत्तेन वेद्धव्यं शरवत्तन्मयो भवेत् ॥

मुण्डकोपनिषत्.

† दृष्टिं ज्ञानमयीं कृत्वा पश्येद्ब्रह्ममयं जगत् ।
सा दृष्टिः परमोदारा न नासाग्रावलोकिनी ॥
दृष्टिदर्शनदृश्यानां विरामो यत्र वा भवेत् ।
दृष्टिस्तत्रैव कर्तव्या न नासाग्रावलोकिनी ॥
चित्तादिसर्वभावेषु ब्रह्मत्वेनैव भावनात् ।
निरोधः सर्ववृत्तीनां प्राणायामः स उच्यते ॥

अपरोक्षानुभूतिः.

CDLXII—CDLXIII.

THE emptying (the mind) of the whole of illusion is the true *rechaka* (the process of emptying the lungs of the air they contain); the full realization of the idea 'I am *Brahman*' is the true *puraka* (the process of filling the lungs with air drawn in from without); and the firm steady sustenance of the mind on this conviction is the true *Kumbhaka* (the retention of the air inhaled). This is the true *Prâṇâyâma* of the enlightened; fools find it only in torturing the nose.*

Aparokshânubhuti.

CDLXIV—CDLXVI.

HIM death never desires to overpower who wears not on his heart the badge of that necklace which has the vices for pearls held together by the thread of unbroken 'latent desires'. Death overpowers him not whom anger, the fire (*vadavânala*) burning at the bottom of the ocean, this body, and parching up the waters of discrimination, has no power to affect. The oil-mill presses the mixed heap of hard sesamum-seeds into an indiscriminate mass ;—death overpowers him not who is not similarly pressed by the bodiless god, Cupid, into a mass, all indiscriminate and confused.†

Yogavâsishtha.

---

* निषेधनं प्रपञ्चस्य रेचकाख्यः समीरणः ।
ब्रह्मैवास्मीति या वृत्तिः पूरको वायुरीरितः ॥
ततस्तद्वृत्तिनैश्चल्यं कुम्भकः प्राणसंयमः ।
अयं चापि प्रबुद्धानामज्ञानां घ्राणपीडनम् ॥

अपरोक्षानुभूतिः.

† दोषमुक्ताफलप्रोता वासनातन्तुसन्ततिः ।
हृदि न ग्रथिता यस्य मृत्युस्तं न जिघांसति ॥
पीताशेषविवेकाम्बुः शरीराम्भोधिवाडवः ।
न निर्दहति यं कोपस्तं मृत्युर्न जिघांसति ॥
यन्त्रं तिलानां कठिनं राशिमुग्रमिवाकुलम् ।
यं पीडयति नानङ्गस्तं मृत्युर्न जिघांसति ॥

योगवासिष्ठम्.

CDLXVII.

AROUSE the mind if it fall into lethargy! pacify it back into its place if it run out; persuade it by proper knowledge if it tend to the objective;—touch it not when it has found the condition of evenness.*

Gaudapâdâchârya.

CDLXVIII.

GNOSIS, the fire which burns up the straw of desire and hope, is all that is meant by the word *Samâdhi*,† not at all the attitude of silence and contemplation.‡

Yogavâsishtha.

CDLXIX.

LET the mind function out into the condition beyond distraction; let it, then, take on the form of the idea 'I am *Brahman*'; and let it lastly subside into entire forgetfulness of all modification whatever. This is the real ecstacy of *gnosis*.§

Aparokshánubhuti.

---

* लये सम्बोधयेच्चित्तं विक्षिप्तं शमयेत् पुनः ।
सकषायं विजानीयात् समप्राप्तं न चालयेत् ॥

गौडपादाचार्यः.

† Rendered into English by the words concentration, abstraction, contemplation, fixing of the mind, and so on. I would prefer the rendering trance, ecstacy, and when we have the adjective *Nirvikalpa* attached to *Samâdhi* I would add the adjective absolute to that rendering.

‡ तत्त्वावबोधो भगवन् सर्वाशातृणपावकः ।
प्रोक्तः समाधिशब्देन न तु तूष्णीमवस्थितिः ॥

योगवासिष्ठम्.

§ निर्विकारतया वृत्त्या ब्रह्माकारतया पुनः ।
वृत्तिविस्मरणं सम्यक् समाधिर्ज्ञानसंज्ञकः ॥

अपरोक्षानुभूतिः.

CDLXX.

WHO sees all acts whatever as being done by nature and nature alone, finds himself ever unrelated to the act.*

Bhagavadgitâ.

CDLXXI.

THE absolute sense of universal Being is realized only then, when consciousness, void of all that it makes conscious, loses itself in the Self, being purified of all relation even like the idea of non-existence.†

Yogavâsishtha.

CDLXXII—CDLXXIII.

THAT *yogin* who finds happiness *within*, has his resting-place *within*, and receives light from *within*; and being *Brahman*, finds supreme extinction in *Brahman*. Sages find extinction in *Brahman* who, free from all dross, ever rise above duality, being all self-control and universal love.‡

Bhâgavatagitâ.

---

* प्रकृत्यैव च कर्माणि क्रियमाणानि सर्वशः ।
यः पश्यति तथात्मानमकर्तारं स पश्यति ॥

भगवद्गीता.

† नूनं चेत्यांशरहिता चिद्यदात्मनि लीयते ।
असद्रूपवदत्यच्छा सत्तासामान्यता तदा ॥

योगवासिष्ठम्.

‡ योऽन्तः सुखोऽन्तरारामस्तथान्तर्ज्योतिरेव यः ।
स योगी ब्रह्मनिर्वाणं ब्रह्मभूतोऽधिगच्छति ॥
लभन्ते ब्रह्म निर्वाणमृषयः क्षीणकल्मषाः ।
छिन्नद्वैधा यतात्मानः सर्वभूतहिते रताः ॥

भगवद्गीता.

CDLXXIV.

WHEN all *thinking* is put out by complete identification with the idea of non-existence, then indeed does consciousness, the common substratum of all, ripen into the absolute sense of universal Being.*

Yogavâsishtha.

CDLXXV.

HE is said to be firm in the Essence who content in Self with Self, clears, oh Son of Pṛthâ! his mind of every trace of desire whatever.†

Bhagavadgitâ.

CDLXXVI.

LET love and its kind by all means remain; their mere existence can certainly give no offence; for *Âvidyâ*, the she-serpent now deprived of her poisonous fangs, is powerless to do any harm.‡

In the Jivanmuktiviveka.

---

* यदा सङ्क्षीयते चित्तमभावात्यन्तभावनात् ।
चित्सामान्यस्वरूपस्य सत्तासामान्यता तदा ॥

योगवासिष्ठम्.

† प्रजहाति यदा कामान्सर्वान्पार्थ मनोगतान् ।
आत्मन्येवात्मना तुष्टः स्थितप्रज्ञस्तदोच्यते ॥

भगवद्गीता.

‡ रागादयः सन्तु कामं न तद्भावोऽपराध्यति ।
उत्खातदंष्ट्रोरगवदविद्या किं करिष्यति ॥

जीवन्मुक्तिविवेकः.

CDLXXVII.

ENJOYMENT well enjoyed through *gnosis* conduces to supreme contentment ; the thief, admitted into company with knowledge of him *as thief*, becomes more a friend than a foe.*

Yogavâsishtha.

CDLXXVIII.

THE knower of the Essence, enjoying all pleasures of the senses, and also realizing the bliss of *Brahman*, may derive both temporal as well as spiritual pleasure even like one having knowledge of two languages.†

Panchadas'i.

CDLXXIX.

I believe him liberated (for ever) who performs every act, without the idea of his doing it, taking it to be only a part of the multifurious spontaneous action of nature (one with his own self).‡

Yogavâsishtha.

---

* परिज्ञायोपभुक्तो हि भोगो भवति तुष्टये ।
विज्ञाय सेवितश्चौरो मैत्रीमेति न चौरताम् ॥

योगवासिष्ठम्.

† भुञ्जानो विषयानन्दं ब्रह्मानन्दं च तत्त्ववित् ।
द्विभाषाभिज्ञवद्विद्यादुभौ लौकिकवैदिकौ ॥

पञ्चदशी.

‡ इमं विश्वपरिस्पन्दं करोमीत्यस्तवासनम् ।
प्रवर्तते यः कार्येषु स मुक्त इति मे मतिः ॥

योगवासिष्ठम्.

CDLXXX—CDLXXXI.

FIXED abode, desire of fine pots etc., for use, laying by a store, the taking of pupils, sleeping by day, vain talk ;—these six degrade the ascetic into bondage. That mendicant falls in no time who consciously parts with his semen and who begins to lay by a store of wealth.*

Smṛti.

CDLXXXII—CDLXXXIII.

THE woman addicted to another, never ceases to taste the elixir of her lover's company, even when all intent on the discharge of her household duties. The wise finding sweet rest in the supreme undefiled Essence, continue for ever to enjoy it within, though going in the ways of the world, without.†

Panchadas'i.

CDLXXXIV.

RELATE thyself not with the future, nor with what has gone by, live the present out with smiling heart.‡

Yogavâsistha.

---

* आसनं पात्रलोभश्च संचयः शिष्यसंग्रहः ।
दिवा स्वापो वृथालापो यतेर्बन्धकराणि षट् ॥

मेधातिथिः.

पतत्यसौ ध्रुवं भिक्षुर्यस्य भिक्षोर्द्वयं भवेत् ।
धीपूर्वं रेतउत्सर्गो द्रव्यसंग्रह एव च ॥

स्मृतिः.

† परव्यसनिनी नारी व्यग्रापि गृहकर्मणि ।
तदेवास्वादयत्यन्तः परसङ्गरसायनम् ॥
एवं तत्त्वे परे शुद्धे धीरो विश्रान्तिमागतः ।
तदेवास्वादयत्यन्तर्बहिर्व्यवहरन्नपि ॥

पञ्चदशी.

‡ भविष्यं नानुसन्धत्ते नातीतं चिन्तयत्यसौ ।
वर्तमाननिमेषन्तु हसन्नेवानुवर्त्तते ॥

योगवासिष्ठम्.

CDLXXXV.

AS fire well-lighted burns the fuel to ashes, so does the fire of *gnosis* reduce, oh *Arjuna*! all *Karma* whatever to the merest dust.*

Bhagavadgitâ.

CDLXXXVI.

THE consciousness of 'self' implied in the 'ego,' the subject, and the consciousness of 'belonging' implied in the 'mine' attached to objects ;—when both these consciousnesses (so to speak) are emptied of all content whatever, then indeed does one become the *knower* of Self.†

Upadeśasâhasri.

CDLXXXVII.

THUS the *araṇi*-wood, this self, being constantly worked upon with this other piece of wood, contemplation, there arises the flame of *gnosis* burning up all ignorance whatever.‡

Âtmabodha.

---

* यथैधांसि समिद्धोऽग्निर्भस्मसात्कुरुतेऽर्जुन ।
ज्ञानाग्निः सर्वकर्माणि भस्मसात्कुरुते तथा ॥

भगवद्गीता.

† अहमित्यात्मधीर्या च ममेत्यात्मीयधीरपि ।
अर्थशून्ये यदा यस्य स आत्मज्ञो भवेत्तदा ॥

उपदेशसाहस्री.

‡ एवमात्मारणौ ध्यानमथने संततं कृते ।
उदितावगतिर्ज्वाला सर्वाज्ञानेन्धनं दहेत् ॥

आत्मबोधः.

CDLXXXVIII.

HE enjoys the ecstacy of absolute trance who, in consequence of the absorbing pleasure of self-realization, rises above all such means as words and objects, and ever stands like the jet of a lamp in some place protected from the breeze.*

Dṛgdṛśyaviveka.

CDLXXXIX.

THE liberated is ever that Being who is the goal of all philosophic reasoning, who is the conviction of every *heart*, who is the All, who is everywhere, who is everything.†

Yogavâsishtha.

CDXC.

HE is liberated even against his wish who gains that full consciousness of self which dispels the illusion identifying self with the body;—consciousness as strong and firm as the knowledge he had while under the illusion.‡

Upadeśasâhasri.

---

* स्वानुभूतिरसावेशाद्दृश्यशब्दावुपेक्षितुः ।
निर्विकल्पः समाधिः स्यान्निवातस्थितदीपवत् ॥

दृग्दृश्यविवेकः.

† यस्सर्वशास्त्रसिद्धान्तो यस्सर्वहृदयानुगम् ।
यत्सर्वं सर्वगं सार्वं यत्तत्तस्तदसौ स्थितः ॥

योगवासिष्ठम्.

‡ देहात्मज्ञानवज्ज्ञानं देहात्मज्ञानबाधकम् ।
आत्मन्येव भवेद्यस्य स नेच्छन्नपि मुच्यते ॥

उपदेशसाहस्री.

CDXCI.

CAPABLE of distinguishing good from evil, ever in supreme peace gained through *gnosis*, cured of its native restlessness, my mind stands, oh sage! in perfect calm.*

Yogavâsishtha.

CDXCII.

HALF of ignorance is destroyed by free exchange of thought, half of the remainder is dispelled by application to philosophy, the rest fades away in the light of self-reflection.†

Yogavâsishtha.

CDXCIII.

IDENTIFICATION with ignorance resulting in obscuration (of the light of Self) disappears with the rise of *gnosis*; the distracting power of ignorance awaits fulfilment of the causes governing the present embodiment.‡

Panchadaśi.

---

* सारासारपरिच्छेदि बोधाद्विश्रान्तिमागतम् ।
निरस्तचापलं शान्तं सुस्थिरं मे मुने मनः ॥

योगवासिष्ठम्.

† अर्धं मिथः सङ्कथया भागः शास्त्रविचारणैः ।
आत्मप्रत्ययतः शिष्टमविद्याया निवर्तते ॥

योगवासिष्ठम्.

‡ अविद्यावृतितादात्म्ये विद्ययैव विनश्यतः ।
विक्षेपस्य स्वरूपं तु प्रारब्धक्षयमीक्षते ॥

पञ्चदशी.

V.—LIBERATION.

CDXCIV—CDXCVI.

BOW to me, this Self, void of consciousness and that which it makes conscious, void of subject and object, of all names whatever ;—self-illumined for once and for ever. Hail again to me, all rest and peace, the high mountain of supreme bliss, smiling under the sky cleared of all clouds of egoism, fresh after complete extinction of the wild, devastating conflagration of hope. To the lamp of love burning bright with its wick of spontaneous ideas without any material oil ;—to the light of inner consciousness, the self-sustained sustainer of the intellect and all that depends on it ;—right hearty welcome, right joyous greeting !*

Yogavâsishtha.

CDXCVII.

WHEN he realises all and every distinction of being as fused into one supreme unity, then, indeed, does he get that expansion which easily makes him *Brahman*.†

Bhaguvadgitâ.

---

* चिचैत्यद्रष्टृदृश्यादिनामभिर्वर्जितात्मने ।
स्वयं सकृद्विभाताय मह्यमस्मै नमोनमः ॥
गताहङ्कारमेघाय शान्ताशादाववन्हये ।
मह्यमानन्दशैलाय विश्रान्ताय नमोनमः ॥
अस्नेहस्नेहदीपाय वृत्तिनिष्क्रान्तवर्तिने ।
स्वभावाधारधीराय चिद्दीपाय नमोनमः ॥

योगवासिष्ठम्.

† यदा भूतपृथग्भावमेकस्थमनुपश्यति ।
तत एव च विस्तारं ब्रह्म सम्पद्यते तदा ॥

भगवद्गीता.

CDXCVIII.

SUBJECT, object, instrument, time, space, categories, being, non-being, phenomena, all are *forms* of that earth which is the blessed Self.*

Yogavâsishtha.

CDXCIX—D.

LIGHTNESS, health, peace, beauty and grace, melodious voice, profuse fragrance, scanty discharge in obeying calls of nature ;—these signify the first-fruits of *Yoga*. The resplendent ball (of gold) encrusted with dust shines in native lustre, on being carefully washed ; the self having regained it Self shines alone in the eternal bliss of supreme fulfilment.†

S'vetâs'vataropanishad.

DI.

AS the sword flashes out of its sheath before the eye in dream, transcending the scheme of all causation, so is the *knower* all self-effulgent (transcending the five sheaths‡ and standing above all causation).§

Upades'asâhasri.

---

* मातृमेयप्रमाणादि देशकालौ दिगादि च ।
भावाभावविवर्तादि शिवपङ्कमयात्मकम् ॥

योगवासिष्ठम्.

† लघुत्वमारोग्यमलोलुपत्वं वर्णः प्रसादः स्वरसौष्ठवं च ।
गन्धः शुभो मूत्रपुरीषमल्पं योगप्रवृत्तिं प्रथमां वदन्ति ॥
यथैव बिम्बं मृदयोपलिप्तं तजोमयं भ्राजते तत् सुधातम् ।
तद्वदात्मतत्त्वं प्रसमीक्ष्य देही एकः कृतार्थो भवते वीतशोकः ॥

श्वेताश्वतरोपनिषत्.

‡ Material, vital, sensual, intellectual, and semi-spiritual (*anna*, *prâṇa*, *manas*, *vijnâna*, *ânanda*).

§ कोषादिव विनिष्कृष्टः कार्यकारणवर्जितः ।
यथासिर्दृश्यते स्वप्ने तद्वद्बोद्धा स्वयंप्रभः ॥

उपदेशसाहस्री.

DII.

THOU mayest realize the distinction between this world and *Brahman* to be as unsubstantial as the distinction between void and *Âkâs'a.**

Yogavâsishtha.

DIII.

THOSE are the enlightened great souls of this world who happen to be firmly fixed in eternal unborn evenness; the world can not even dream of it.†

Gaudapâdâchârya.

DIV.

SIGHT of the Supreme breaks asunder the knot (of egoism) in the heart, dispels all doubts, extinguishes all *Karma.*‡

Muṇḍakopanishad.

---

* शून्यत्वाकाशयोर्भेदो यादृशोऽवगतस्त्वया ।
भेदं निरात्मकं विद्धि तादृशं ब्रह्मसर्गयोः ॥

योगवासिष्ठम्.

† अजे साम्ये तु ये केचिद्भविष्यन्ति सुनिश्चिताः ।
ते हि लोके महाज्ञानास्तच्च लोको न गाहते ॥

गौडपादाचार्याः.

‡ भिद्यते हृदयग्रन्थिश्छिद्यन्ते सर्वसंशयाः ।
क्षीयन्ते चास्य कर्माणि तस्मिन्दृष्टे परावरे ॥

मुण्डकोपनिषत्.

DV.

THE blindest sensualist finds in his mother the irremovable bar to the excess of his indulgence; the man of the sharpest intellect forgets himself in the ultimate resort of all thought and all bliss, *viz. Brahman.**

Vivekachudâmaṇi.

DVI.

THEREFORE, the *knower* of *Brahman* finishing off all learning, should wish to be strong in the Self, and finishing off even this strength as well as that learning he should try to become the silent one. Finishing off learning and strength and silence he becomes the true *Brâhmaṇa*, the real *knower* of *Brahman*. What, indeed, makes the *Brâhmaṇa*? Whatever may make the *Brâhmaṇa*, he cannot be other than the one thus described; all beside is vain and worthless.†

Bṛhadâraṇyakopanishad.

DVII.

POWDER of the *kataka*-wood‡ put into water settles down with the mud that makes it impotable. *Gnosis,*

---

* अत्यन्तकामुकस्यापि वृत्तिः कुण्ठति मातरि ।
तथैव ब्रह्मणि ज्ञाते पूर्णानन्दे मनीषिणः ॥

विवेकचूडामणिः.

† तस्माद् ब्राह्मणः पाण्डित्यं निर्विद्य बाल्येन तिष्ठासेद्बाल्यञ्च पाण्डित्यञ्च निर्विद्याथ मुनिरमौनञ्च मौनञ्च निर्विद्याथ ब्राह्मणः स ब्राह्मणः केन स्याद्येन स्यात्तेनेदृश एवातोऽन्यदार्तम् ।

बृहदारण्यकोपनिषत्.

‡ Largely used in Benares and other places when the waters of the Ganges become turbid during the rains.

constantly put in, disappears with the ignorance which renders the soul all turbid, leaving it in the native purity of it-Self.*

Átmabodha.

DVIII—DIX.

NOTHING moves him (to love or hate) who finds all beings in himself and himself in all beings. What can delusion or sorrow mean then? when to the *knower* realizing unity of the All, every particle has become his Self.†

Is'opanishad.

DX.

GNOSIS having shown the absolute non-existence of the objective, supreme peace of liberation is fully realized in the mind's being wiped clean of all and every object whatever.‡

Panchadas'i.

---

* अज्ञानकलुषं जीवं ज्ञानाभ्यासाद्वि निर्मलम् ।
कृत्वाज्ञानं स्वयं नश्येज्जलं कतकरेणुवत् ॥

आत्मबोधः.

† यस्तु सर्वाणि भूतान्यात्मन्येवानुपश्यति ।
सर्वभूतेषु चात्मानं ततो न विजुगुप्सते ॥
यस्मिन्सर्वाणि भूतान्यात्मैवाभूद्विजानतः ।
तत्र को मोहः कः शोक एकत्वमनुपश्यतः ॥

ईशोपनिषत्.

‡ दृश्यं नास्तीति बोधेन मनसो दृश्यमार्जनम् ।
संपन्नं चेत्तदुत्पन्ना परा निर्वाणनिर्वृतिः ॥

पञ्चदशी.

DXI.

EXPERIENCE in the light of *gnosis* dissolving every impression it may leave behind,—this sleep in waking,—is the real nature of those who *know*; liberation is only the highest development of this nature.*

Yogavâsishtka.

DXII.

SAID Yâjnavalkya:—This is not the Self, this is not the Self; the incomprehensible is never comprehended, the indissoluble is never dissolved, the unconditioned is never conditioned, the unpained is never pained, never put out;—thou oh Janaka! hast realized entire fearlessness.†

Bṛhadâraṇyakopanishad.

DXIII.

THE night of all beings is wakefulness of the real sage; the wakefulness of all beings is the night of the silent seer.‡

Bhagavadgitâ.

---

* यज्जाग्रति सुषुप्तत्वं बोधादरसवासनम् ।
ते स्वभावं विदुस्तज्ज्ञा मुक्तिस्तत्परिणामिता ॥

योगवासिष्ठम्.

† स एष नेतिनेत्यात्मागृह्यो न हि गृह्यतेऽशीर्यो न हि शीर्यतेऽसङ्गो न हि सज्यतेऽसितो न व्यथते न रिष्यत्यभयं वै जनक प्राप्तोऽसीति होवाच याज्ञवल्क्यः ॥

बृहदारण्यकोपनिषत्.

‡ या निशा सर्वभूतानां तस्यां जागर्ति संयमी ।
यस्यां जाग्रति भूतानि सा निशा पश्यतो मुनेः ॥

भगवद्गीता.

DXIV.

THE bliss of *Brahman*!—speech and mind fall back baffled and abashed; all fear vanishes in the *knowing* of that bliss.*

Taittiriyopanishad.

DXV.

THE silent one, the *knower* ever resting in the Self, may walk, stand, sit, lie down, or do anything at his sweet will.†

Vivekachudâmaṇi.

DXVI.

I do not see, for, I have no eyes; without ears, how can I hear? I cannot speak, for, I have no speech; without mind how could I find the world of mind?‡

Upades'asâhasri.

DXVII.

THERE is none superior to me in self-knowledge, none inferior to me in ignorance; who *unknowingly* knows thus, is the greatest *knower* of *Brahman*.§

Naishkarmyasiddhi.

---

* यतो वाचो निवर्तन्ते अप्राप्य मनसा सह ।
आनन्दं ब्रह्मणो विद्वान्न बिभेति कुतश्चन ॥
तैत्तिरीयोपनिषद्.

† गच्छंस्तिष्ठन्नुपविशञ्छयानो वान्यथापि वा ।
यथेच्छया वसेद्विद्वानात्मारामः सदा मुनिः ॥
विवेकचूडामणिः.

‡ अचक्षुष्ट्वान्न दृष्टिर्मे तथाश्रोत्रस्य का श्रुतिः ।
अवाक्त्वान्न तु वक्तिः स्यादमनस्त्वान्मतिः कुतः ॥
उपदेशसाहस्री.

§ नेहात्मविन्मदन्योऽस्ति न मत्तोऽज्ञोऽस्ति कश्चन ।
इत्यजानन् विजानाति यः स ब्रह्मविदुत्तमः ॥
नैष्कर्म्यसिद्धिः.

DXVIII.

NEITHER knowable nor unknowable; neither spoken nor unspoken; neither liked nor disliked; impossible of retaining in any mental presentation; nay not possible to fix in contemplation even for a moment; all bliss through and through; beautiful in the deep sense of ecstatic self-realization; this my-Self wonderfully dissolves the world in the sudden flash of its abundant light.*

Svârâjyasiddhi.

DXIX.

SEPARATE, unique, one, multifarious, knowable, knower, motive, mover,—these and other imaginings of the same kind, where could they find room in me all One?†

Upade'sasâhasri.

DXX.

EGOISM having disengaged itself from the body, and having been dissolved in the light of Supreme Self, the mind stands in blissful trance wherever it goes, whatever it directs itself to.‡

Drgdr'syaviveka.

---

* न वेद्यो नावेद्यः स्वरसमतिहृद्यः सुखघनो
न गद्यो नापोद्यो न पुनरुपरोध्यः कथमपि ।
न हेयो नादेयो न पुनरपिधेयः क्षणमहो
स्फुरन्नात्मास्माकं जगदिदमकस्मात्तिरयति ॥

स्वाराज्यसिद्धिः.

† भेदोऽभेदस्तथा चैको नाना चेति विकल्पितम् ।
ज्ञेयं ज्ञाता गतिर्गन्ता मय्येकास्मिन्कुतो भवेत् ॥

उपदेशसाहस्री.

‡ देहाभिमाने गलिते विज्ञाते परमात्मनि ।
यत्र यत्र मनो याति तत्र तत्र समाधयः ॥

दृग्दृश्यविवेकः.

DXXI.

(KNOW that to be the best *Yoga*) wherein the mind held fast in steady application finds supreme rest, wherein seeing Self with Self (in all things whatever) it loses itself in the bliss of Self.*

Bhagavadgitâ.

DXXII.

THE native form of the subject, highly transcendent like *Âkâśa*, self-illumined for once and for ever, unborn, one, immutable, unconditioned, all-pervading, without a second;—I am this, the ever liberated word of glory.†

Upadeśasâhasri.

DXXIII.

ALL beings in Self, and Self in all beings:—thus sees he who, with his Self full of *Yoga*, has acquired that eye which is even to all.‡

Bhagavadgitâ.

---

* यत्रोपरमते चित्तं निरुद्धं योगसेवया ।
यत्र चैवात्मनात्मानं पश्यन्नात्मनि तुष्यति ॥

भगवद्गीता।

† दृशिस्वरूपं गगनोपमं परं सकृद्विभातं त्वजमेकमक्षरम् ।
अलेपकं सर्वगतं यदद्वयं तदेव चाहं सततं विमुक्तओं ॥

उपदेशसाहस्री।

‡ सर्वभूतस्थमात्मानं सर्वभूतानि चात्मनि ।
ईक्षते योगयुक्तात्मा सर्वत्र समदर्शनः ॥

भगवद्गीता।

DXXIV.

HE has had a dip in the holy waters of all sacred rivers ; he has given the whole earth in pious gift ; he has offered a thousand sacrifices ; he has satisfied all the gods in heaven ; he has lifted his ancesters out of the circle of birth and death ; he deserves worship of all the three worlds ;—the man whose mind has, even for a moment, tasted of peace in the absorbing idea of *Brahman.**

Miscellaneous.

DXXV—DXXVII.

NEITHER love nor hate, neither ambition nor illusion, neither pride nor the least tinge of jealousy, no good, spiritual or temperal, no desire, no liberation ;—I am none of these, I am all bliss, the bliss all eternal consciousness. Holiness or unholiness, happiness or misery, incantation or holy pilgrimage, scripture or sacrifice, none of these belong to me ; not even the enjoyed, the enjoyer, or the sense of enjoyment ; I am all bliss, the bliss all eternal consciousness. Death I fear not, caste I respect not, father, mother, nay even birth, I know not, relatives, friends I

---

* स्नातं तेन समस्ततीर्थसलिले दत्तापि सर्वावनि-
र्यज्ञानां च कृतं सहस्रमखिला देवाश्च संपूजिताः ।
संसाराच्च समुद्धृताः स्वपितरस्त्रैलोक्यपूज्योऽप्यसौ
यस्य ब्रह्मविचारणे क्षणमपि स्थैर्यं मनः प्राप्नुयात् ॥

प्रास्ताविकः.

recognize not, teacher and pupil I own not ;—I am all bliss, the bliss all eternal consciousness.*

S'ankarâchârya.

DXXVIII.

I am *Brahman*, not at all of the world, never apart from *Brahman* ; I am not the body, nor have I any body whatever ;—I am the unconditioned, eternal, One.†

S'ankarâchârya.

DXXIX.

THIS mortal habitat brought about or carried off by chance :—the accomplished, inasmuch as he has found him-Self, recks not whether it stands or falls, even like the

---

* न मे द्वेषरागौ न मे लोभमोहौ
मदो नैव मे नैव मात्सर्यभानम् ।
न धर्मो न चार्थो न कामो न मोक्ष-
श्चिदानन्दरूपः शिवोऽहं शिवोऽहम् ॥
न पुण्यं न पापं न सौख्यं न दुःखं
न मन्त्रो न तीर्थं न वेदा न यज्ञाः ।
अहं भोजनं नैव भोज्यं न भोक्ता
चिदानन्दरूपः शिवोऽहं शिवोऽहम् ॥
न मे मृत्युशङ्का न मे जातिभेदः
पिता नैव मे नैव माता न जन्म ।
न बन्धुर्न मित्रं गुरुर्नैव शिष्य-
श्चिदानन्दरूपः शिवोऽहं शिवोऽहम् ॥

आत्मषट्कम्.

† ब्रह्मैवाहं न संसारी न चाहं ब्रह्मणः पृथक् ।
नाहं देहो न मे देहः केवलोऽहं सनातनः ॥

आत्मचिन्तनम्.

drunkard blind with intoxication who recks not whether the cloth he wears remains or falls away.*

Bhâgavata.

DXXX.

WHO, being full of unity, sees not, as in sleep, the least trace of duality, though seeing it in entire wakefulness; who though acting is, for the same reason, entirely at rest;— he and no one else is verily the true knower of Self.†

Upades'asâhasri.

DXXXI.

WHO feels not any attachment for the senses or objects peculiar to the senses, nor for any action whatever, and who has renounced all mental creation of every description; he has attained the highest pitch of *Yoga*.‡

Bhagavadgitâ.

---

* देहं च नश्वरमवस्थितमुत्थितं वा
सिद्धो न पश्यति यतोऽध्यगमत्स्वरूपम् ।
दैवादुपेतमथ दैववशादपेतं
वासो यथा परिकृतं मदिरामदान्धः ॥

भागवतम्.

† सुषुप्तवज्जाग्रति यो न पश्यति द्वयं तु पश्यन्नपि चाद्वयत्वतः ।
तथा च कुर्वन्नपि निष्क्रियश्च यः स आत्मविन्नान्य इतीह निश्चयः ॥

उपदेशसाहस्री.

‡ यदा हि नेन्द्रियार्थेषु न कर्मस्वनुषज्जते ।
सर्वसंकल्पसन्न्यासी योगारूढस्तदोच्यते ॥

भगवद्गीता.

DXXXII—DXXXIII.

HE is all taste and refinement, yet all insipid; he is merciless yet fondness itself towards relatives; he is cruel yet all compassion; he is beyond desire, yet deep in the whirl of all desire. All care and anxiety without like the rest of Mankind, yet all quiet and calm within, he stands as if possessed, though ever unpossessed.*

Yogavâsishtha.

DXXXIV.

REGALING all content in the nectar of *gnosis*, fully satisfied in supreme fulfilment of every duty, there remains nothing for the *yogin* to do; if anything remain, he must be just so many removes behind *gnosis*.†

In the Jivanmuktiviveka.

DXXXV.

THE least of a thing is greatest if it comes without trouble to any one, without seeking it of the wicked, and without the least pang at heart.‡

Mahâbhârata.

---

* रसिकोऽत्यन्तविरसो निर्घृणो बन्धुवत्सलः ।
निर्दयोऽत्यन्तकरुणो वितृष्णस्तृष्णयान्वितः ॥
बहिः सर्वसमाचारमन्तः सर्वार्थशीतलम् ।
नित्यमन्तरनाविष्ट आविष्ट इव तिष्ठति ॥

योगवासिष्ठम्.

† ज्ञानामृतेन तृप्तस्य कृतकृत्यस्य योगिनः ।
नैवास्ति किञ्चित्कर्तव्यमस्ति चेन्न स तत्त्ववित् ॥

जीवन्मुक्तिविवेकः.

‡ अकृत्वा परसन्तापमगत्वा खलमन्दिरम् ।
अक्लेशयित्वा चात्मानं यदल्पमपि तद्बहु ॥

महाभारतम्.

DXXXVI.

THE cycle of strife and struggle will place *Brahman* in the mouth of all; none, oh Maitreya! will show it in the act, being really intent on the pleasures of sex and stomach.*

In the Jivanmuktiviveka.

DXXXVII.

I am *Brahman*, I am the creator, I am the enjoyer;—those who thus know are lost to *gnosis* as also to the purifying forms of external worship;—they are on the highway to materialistic Atheism.†

Upades'asâhasri.

DXXXVIII.

OH Gârgi! who performs the sacrifice, who undergoes the severest penance even for several thousands of years, all without knowledge of this Immutable Essence, meets only with that good which is sure to end. Who passes away, dear Gârgi! from this world, without knowledge of this Immutable Essence, goes away, alas! with the tight bond of narrow-

---

* सर्वे ब्रह्म वदिष्यन्ति संप्राप्ते तु कलौ युगे ।
नानुतिष्ठन्ति मैत्रेय शिश्नोदरपरायणाः ॥

जीवन्मुक्तिविवेकः.

† अहं ब्रह्मास्मि कर्ता च भोक्ता चास्मीति ये विदुः।
ते नष्टा ज्ञानकर्मभ्यां नास्तिकाः स्युर्न संशयः ॥

उपदेशसाहस्री.

ness about his heart ; he alone who passes away in the knowledge of this Immutable Essence is the real *Brâhmaṇa.**

Bṛhadâraṇyakopanishad.

DXXXIX.

THE heart of the wicked never melts into goodness, though he should be deep immersed in the *Vadânta* ; not a particle of the Mainâka† is seen to soften where he hides himself from eternity under the waters of the deep.‡

Jagannâth.

DXL.

ALWAYS at their best while talking of *Brahman*, but without the heart having at all *become* It, being all coloured with love of the world ;—these too, are ignorant fools of the first degree, never free from the circle of death and birth.§

Aparokshânubhuti.

---

* यो वा एतदक्षरं गार्ग्यविदित्वास्मिँल्लोके जुहोति यजते तपस्तप्यते बहूनि वर्षसहस्राण्यन्तवदेवास्य तद्भवति यो वा एतदक्षरं गार्ग्यविदित्वास्माल्लोकात्प्रैति स कृपणोऽथ य एतदक्षरं गार्गि विदित्वास्माल्लोकात्प्रैति स ब्राह्मणः ॥

बृहदारण्यकोपनिषत्.

† Son of the Himálaya ; he deserted his father and took refuge under the waters of the ocean when Indra began to cut off the wings of mountains with his thunderbolt.

‡ निष्णातोऽपि हि वेदान्ते साधुत्वं नैति दुर्जनः ।
चिरं जलनिधौ मग्नो मैनाक इव मार्दवम् ॥

जगन्नाथः.

§ कुशला ब्रह्मवार्तायां वृत्तिहीनाः सुरागिणः ।
तेप्यज्ञानतमा नूनं पुनरायान्ति यान्ति च ॥

अपरोक्षानुभूतिः.

DXLI.

WHO does *not* know, *knows*; who *knows*, does *not* know; It is *known* to those who do *not* know, It is *not* known to those who *know*.*

Kenopanishad.

DXLII.

THE laddle helps to prepare a variety of viands, but it never knows the taste of any one of them: he knows all the four *Vedas*, and Institutes of Duty without end, but the poor thing knows not the essence of them all—*Brahman*.†

Uttaragitâ.

DXLIII—DXLIV.

THAT deluded soul is verily a hypocrite who, holding the active organs in full control, sits mentally meditating upon objects of sense. He, oh Arjuna! is the best of all who excersing mental control over the senses, leaves their activity to work itself out in the way of *Karma*, thus ever remaining unattached (to the result).‡

Bhagavadgitâ.

---

* यस्यामतं तस्य मतं मतं यस्य न वेद सः ।
अविज्ञातं विजानतां विज्ञातमविजानताम् ॥

केनोपनिषत्.

† अधीत्य चतुरो वेदान्धर्मशास्त्राण्यनेकशः ।
ब्रह्मतत्त्वं न जानाति दर्वी पाकरसं यथा ॥

उत्तरगीता.

‡ कर्मेन्द्रियाणि संयम्य य आस्ते मनसा स्मरन् ।
इन्द्रियार्थान्विमूढात्मा मिथ्याचारः स उच्यते ॥
यस्त्विन्द्रियाणि मनसा नियम्यारभतेऽर्जुन ।
कर्मेन्द्रियैः कर्मयोगमसक्तः स विशिष्यते ॥

भगवद्गीता.

DXLV.

ATTACHMENT to any one of the many fields which the mind visits for exercise is the surest sign of ignorance; greenness is certainly impossible in the tree that conceals a consuming fire in its hollow.*

Naishkarmyasiddhi.

DXLVI—DXLVIII.

THE swimmer, having safely carried many to the other side of the stream, is drawn into the whirlpool, and is carried beyond all help. Those, on the other side, who feel grateful for his help, pity him, others pass on in indifference. The *knower* caught into the whirlpool of words and technicalities, those pity who having reached the other side of all words and all forms feel yet grateful for his help.†

Âtmapurâṇa.

---

* रागो लिङ्गमबोधस्य चित्तव्यायामभूमिषु ।
कुतः शाड्वलता तस्य यस्याग्निः कोटरे तरोः ॥

नैष्कर्म्यसिद्धिः.

† तारयित्वा परं पारं यथा यद्वद्धि तारकः ।
आवर्ते पतितो नैवमुद्धर्तुमिह शक्यते ॥
परतीरे गता ये स्युरुपकारस्य बोधकाः ।
शोचन्ति तत्र तं त्वन्ये गच्छन्ति च यथासुखम् ॥
शब्दाद्यावर्तपतितो विद्वानपि तथैव सः ।
शोच्यतेऽत्रोपकारज्ञैः परपारमुपागतैः ॥

आत्मपुराणम्.

DXLIX.

THAT knower of Self who yet deals in give and take has not graduated himself for Liberation; *Brahman* has vomitted him out for ever.*

Upades'asâhasri.

DL.

THE gods know him to be a *Brâhmaṇa* who, without any upper garment or any clothing whatever, sleeping upon no bed, and using nothing but his hand for a pillow, remains ever at peace (within and without).†

Śmṛti.

DLI.

EVEN animals and *Mlechhas*, embodied or disembodied, are all undoubtedly liberated in full, if they have attained to the condition of this *gnosis.*‡

Yogavâsishtha.

---

* आत्मज्ञस्यापि यस्य स्याद्धानोपादानता यदि ।
न मोक्षार्हः स विज्ञेयो वान्तोऽसौ ब्रह्मणा ध्रुवम् ॥

उपदेशसाहस्री.

† अनुत्तरीयवसनमनुपस्तीर्णशायिनम् ।
बाहूपधायिनं शान्तं तं देवा ब्राह्मणं विदुः ॥

व्यासः.

‡ प्राप्ता ज्ञानदशामेतां पशुम्लेच्छादयोऽपि ये ।
सदेहा वाप्यदेहा वा ते मुक्ता नात्र संशयः ॥

योगवासिष्ठम्.

DLII.

THE wise grieves not, having seen the unbodied Self pervading all mortal forms, ever great, all-embracing.*

Kathopanishad.

DLIII—DLV.

AS is the being of things, the void-ness of void, or the being with forms of forms, so is this universe of *chidâkâsa.* That whereof comes the whole universe at the end of sleep, and that wherein it dissolves itself at the moment of rest, is this *chidâkâsa.* Misery overpowers not that ascetic who ever remains in the condition which is being daily experienced between the point where sleep begins and the point where wakefulness ends.†

Yogavâsishtha.

---

* अशरीरं शरीरेष्वनवस्थेष्ववस्थितम् ।
महान्तं विभुमात्मानं मत्वा धीरो न शोचति ॥

कठोपनिषत्.

† यथा भावस्य भावत्वं यथा शून्यस्य शून्यता ।
आकारिणो यथाकारस्तथा चिन्नभसो जगत् ॥
निद्रायां विनिवृत्तायां यतो विश्वं प्रवर्तते ।
निवर्तते च यच्छान्तौ तच्चिदम्बर उच्यते ॥
निद्रादौ जागरस्यान्ते यो भाव उपजायते ।
तं भावं धारयन् योगी न दुःखैरभिभूयते ॥

योगवासिष्ठम्.

DLVI.

THE ring of this cosmos can hardly suffice for the enjoyment of the high-minded knower; the flutter of a tiny fish can produce but a scant ruffle on the surface of the deep.*

Bhartṛhari.

DLVII.

HE who is harmonised in Self, who finds full bliss in Self, and who is all content in Self, has no call of duty (to disturb him).†

Bhagavadgitâ.

DLVIII.

THOUGH taking part in all intercourse of every kind, like all ordinary men, he soars constantly above all beings, conscious or unconscious.‡

Yogavâsishtha.

---

* ब्रह्माण्डमण्डलीमात्रं किं भोगाय मनस्विनः ।
शफरीस्फुरितेनाब्धेः क्षुब्धता जातु जायते ॥

भर्तृहरिः.

† यस्त्वात्मरतिरेव स्यादात्मतृप्तश्च मानवः ।
आत्मन्येव च सन्तुष्टस्तस्य कार्यं न विद्यते ॥

भगवद्गीता.

‡ व्यवहारं यथाप्राप्तं लोकसामान्यमाचरन् ।
चराचरणां भूतानामुपर्येवावतिष्ठते ॥

योगवासिष्ठम्.

DLIX.

IF of he knows his self as the Self, what desire, what object, should burn his body in the fever (of care and anxitey).*

Bṛhadâraṇyakopanishad.

DLX.

WITH mind attuned to Me, with the whole of their vital energy fully harmonised in Me, ever enlightening one another, ever talking of Me, they engage themselves in this pleasing pastime of eternal contentment.†

Bhagavadgitâ.

DLXI.

THINK of It, speak of It, enlighten one another in It;—this is full devotion to the idea of Oneness, this, the wise call study of *Brahman*.‡

Panchadas'i.

---

* आत्मानं चेद्विजानीयादहमस्मीति पूरुषः ।
किमिच्छन् कस्य कामाय शरीरमनुसञ्ज्वरेत् ॥

बृहदारण्यकोपनिषत्.

† मच्चित्ता मद्गतप्राणा बोधयन्तः परस्परम् ।
कथयन्तश्च मां नित्यं तुष्यन्ति च रमन्ति च ॥

भगवद्गीता.

‡ तच्चिन्तनं तत्कथनमन्योन्यं तत्प्रबोधनम् ।
एतदेकपरत्वं हि ब्रह्माभ्यासं विदुर्बुधाः ॥

पञ्चदशी.

DLXII.

LET calamity, oh Lord of the Universe! visit us here, there and everywhere, that we may have the benefit of thy holy presence, and of the (consequent) absence of the necessity of re-entering this world.*

Bhâgavata.

DLXIII.

THE irrevocable love which the indiscriminate have in objects (of sense);—may that very love never fade from my heart while it yet continues to be full of thy holy memory.†

Panchadas'i.

DLXIV.

THE sage reconciled in the perfect rest of Self, freed from the ties (of egoism and ignorance), keeps up strong loving devotion to the mighty one, without any cause whatever, for, the Lord is all love.‡

Bhâgavata.

---

* विपदः सन्तु नः शश्वत्तत्र तत्र जगद्गुरो ।
भवतां दर्शनं यत्स्यादपुनर्भवदर्शनम् ॥

भागवतम्.

† या प्रीतिरविवेकानां विषयेष्वनपायिनी ।
त्वामनुस्मरतः सा मे हृदयान्मापसर्पतु ॥

पञ्चदशी.

‡ आत्मारामापि मुनयो निर्ग्रन्था अप्युरुक्रमे ।
कुर्वन्त्यहैतुकीं भक्तिमित्थंभूतगुणो हरिः ॥

भागवतम्.

DLXV.

GREAT souls, ever at rest in the Self, all light, and standing at the height of development, are always as firm within as mount Meru, though appearing as fickle without as the tip of a feather.*

Yogavâsishtha.

DLXVI.

NEITHER joy nor sorrow, neither movable nor immovably fixed, neither being nor non-being, nay not even the intermediate between these opposites;—so is described the mind of the enlightened.†

Yogavâsishtha.

DLXVII.

THE army engaged in close battle, in a picture, fights all unmoved; the wise, though deep in intercourse with the world, stands equally even in all conditions.‡

Yogavâsishtha.

---

* आत्मारामा महात्मानः प्रबुद्धाः परमोदयाः ।
बहिः पिच्छाग्रतरला अन्तर्मेरुरिवाचलाः ॥

योगवासिष्ठम्.

† नानन्दं न निरानन्दं न चलं नाचलं स्थिरम् ।
न सन्नासन्न चैतेषां मध्यं ज्ञानिमनो विदुः ॥

योगवासिष्ठम्.

‡ चित्रसंगरयुद्धस्य सैन्यस्याक्षुब्धता यथा ।
तथैव समता ज्ञस्य व्यवहारवतोऽपि च ॥

योगवासिष्ठम्.

DLXVIII.

THE Vedas, the *Smṛtis*, constant study of the *Purâṇas*, close application to the subtleties of philosophy;—what do these avail! What, indeed, is the use of that whirl of ceremonial worship which at best lodges the weary soul in some hovel of the village called Heaven! Conscious harmony in the blissful condition of Self, the great-*pralaya*-fire of the net of misery born of the bondage of this world;—all, saving this, are but the toys of (spiritual) pedlary.*

Bhartṛhari.

DLXIX.

CONSCIOUSNESS imagining itself into the act, takes on the result of that act; consciousness not imagining itself into the act, is ever free of the result.†

Yogavâsishtha.

---

* किं वेदैः स्मृतिभिः पुराणपठनैः शास्त्रैर्महाविस्तरैः
स्वर्गग्रामकुटीनिवासफलदैः कर्मक्रियाविभ्रमैः।
मुक्त्वैकं भवबन्धदुःखरचनाविध्वंसकालानलं
स्वात्मानन्दपदप्रवेशकलनं शेषा वणिग्वृत्तयः॥

भर्तृहरिः.

† कर्मकल्पनया संवित्स्वकर्मफलभागिनी।
कर्मकल्पनयोन्मुक्ता न कर्मफलभागिनी॥

योगवासिष्ठम्.

DLXX.

WHERE could that be invoked which fills all space? where is the seat of that which is the seat of all? Of the ever clean, what can be the wash or the offering of honour? To the ever pure, what the drink that purifies within?*

S'ankarâchârya.

DLXXI.

I have no distraction, and therefore no trance; distraction or trance are all incidents of the mind under power of attraction.†

Upades'asâhasri.

DLXXII—DLXXIII.

THE idea which consciousness, at first, imagines, of itself, as its own form, *that* it continues to *be* even to the present day. The same consciousness may, by yet another effort of greater strength, take the opposite form, and so on and on, in proportion to the effort it should put forth.‡

Yogavâsishtha.

---

* पूर्णस्यावाहनं कुत्र सर्वाधारस्य चासनम् ।
स्वच्छस्य पाद्यमर्घ्यं च शुद्धस्याचमनं कुतः ॥

परापूजा.

† विक्षेपो नास्ति यस्मान्मे न समाधिस्ततो मम ।
विक्षेपो वा समाधिर्वा मनसः स्याद्विकारिणः ॥

उपदेशसाहस्री.

‡ यथज्ञानात्मकं रूपं प्रथमं चिन्तितं चिता ।
स्वतोऽहमेव चित्येव तदद्यापि तथास्थितम् ॥
पुनरन्येन यत्नेन तदुत्कृष्टेन सैव चित् ।
शक्ता तदन्यथा कर्तुं यत्नेन महता पुनः ॥

योगवासिष्ठम्.

DLXXIV.

NEITHER teacher nor book, neither pupil nor teaching, neither you nor I, neither this nor that;—the light of Self, intolerant of all doubt whatever, I am all pure bliss, the one *residuum* of the many thus denied.*

S'ankarâchârya.

DLXXV.

HE who relates not his 'ego' with the act as *doer*, nor his mind with the result as *sufferer*, never kills nor does the act even if he should destroy all the three worlds at a stroke.†

Bhagavadgitâ.

DLXXVI.

THE patient *Brâhmaṇa* having known It should harmonise himself in the Self, he should not be deluded away by words; it is mere waste of breath.‡

Bṛhadâraṇyakopanishad.

---

* न शास्ता न शास्त्रं न शिष्यो न शिक्षा
न च त्वं न चाहं न चायं प्रपञ्चः ।
स्वरूपावबोधो विकल्पासहिष्णु-
स्तदेकोऽवशिष्टः शिवः केवलोऽहम् ॥

निर्वाणदशकम्.

† यस्य नाहङ्कृतो भावो बुद्धिर्यस्य न लिप्यते ।
हत्वापि स इमाँल्लोकान्न हन्ति न निबध्यते ॥

भगवद्गीता.

‡ तमेव धीरो विज्ञाय प्रज्ञां कुर्वीत ब्राह्मणः ।
नानुध्यायाद्बहूञ्छब्दान्वाचो विग्लापनं हि तत् ॥

बृहदारण्यकोपनिषत्.

DLXXVII.

THE wise having found the path of *gnosis*, indirect and direct, from the study of books, should cast them away even like straw after thrashing the rice out of it.*

Panchadas'i.

DLXXVIII.

THIS is the truth: I know no change, for, there can be no cause to change, there being all oneness out and out. No spiritual merit or demerit, no liberation or bondage, nor have I any *Varṇa* or *Ás'rama*, for, I have not the body of which these are accidents.†

Upades'asâhasri.

DLXXIX.

S'ANKHYA, S'aiva, Pâncharâtra, Jaina, Mimânsâ, none of these philosophies do I profess; I am that pure con-

---

* ग्रन्थमभ्यस्य मेधावी ज्ञानविज्ञानतत्परः ।
पलालमिव धान्यार्थी त्यजेद्ग्रन्थमशेषतः ॥

पञ्चदशी.

† इदं तु सत्यं मम नास्ति विक्रिया विकारहेतुर्न हि मेऽद्वयत्वतः ।
न पुण्यपापे न च मोक्षबन्धने न चास्ति वर्णाश्रमताशरीरतः ॥

उपदेशसाहस्री.

sciousness, the subject of distinct self-experience, all pure bliss, the one *residuum* of the many thus denied.*

S'ankarâchârya.

DLXXX.

IN the duties of *Varṇa* and *Âsrama* some, in madness others take delight; in child-like innocence some, in stupid indifference others find their meed; lover, re veler, ascetic, to no one grade of life the *knower* confines his choice.†

Svarâjyasiddhi.

DLXXXI.

A perfect fool in one place, all royal splendour in another; at times in fond delusion, at times entire peace and quiet; often in the slothful indifference of the boa; the subject of the highest encomiums in one place, in another all

---

* न साङ्ख्यं न शैवं न तत्पाञ्चरात्रम्
न जैनं न मीमांसकादेर्मतं वा ।
विशिष्टानुभूत्या विशुद्धात्मकत्वात्
तदेकोऽवशिष्टः शिवः केवलोऽहम् ॥

निर्वाणदशकम्.

† केऽपि वर्णाश्रमाचारनिष्ठा मुग्धबालप्रमत्तोपमाश्चापरे ।
रागिणो भोगिनो योगिनश्चेतरे ज्ञानिनां लक्ष्यते नैकरूपा स्थितिः ॥

स्वाराज्यसिद्धिः.

contempt, in a third entirely unnoticed;—thus goes about the wise knower, ever happy in the highest bliss.*

Vivekachudâmaṇi.

DLXXXII.

THE ascetic, not straying away from the path of wisdom, should so conduct himself as men, feeling repelled, should seek not his company.†

Smṛti.

DLXXXIII.

THE ignorant set up this panorama of objects, I wipe it out as often; I have faith in none; I am not affraid of the last penalty of Yama; I hate virtue; Self-satisfaction is all I seek; the whole of my wonderful life spent in cheating the world, none can understand.‡

Svarâjyasiddhi.

---

* क्वचिन्मूढो विद्वान् क्वचिदपि महाराजविभवः
क्वचिद्भ्रान्तः सौम्यः क्वचिदजगराचारकलितः ।
क्वचित्पात्रीभूतः क्वचिदवमतः क्वाप्यविदित-
श्चरत्येवं प्राज्ञः सततपरमानन्दसुखितः ॥

विवेकचूडामणिः.

† तथाचरेत वै योगी सतां धर्ममदूषयन् ।
जना यथावमन्येरन् गच्छेयुर्नैव सङ्गतिम् ॥

स्मृतिः.

‡ मुहुर्मूढैर्न्यस्तं भृशमपलपाम्यर्थनिचयं
न कश्चिद्विश्वास्यो न मम यमदण्डादपि भयम् ।
गुणद्वेषी स्वार्थप्रिय इति जगद्वञ्चनपरं
चरित्रं मे चित्रं क्वचिदपि न कश्चित्कलयति ॥

स्वाराज्यसिद्धिः.

DLXXXIV.

WHAT means self-realization to me, all eternal realization (from end to end); all duties have been done, all wishes have been fulfilled, this is the most sure conviction (of my heart.)*

Panchadaśi.

DLXXXV.

I neither do nor make do, I neither enjoy nor make enjoy, I neither see nor make see; I am the self-effulgent Self unlike every possible name or form.†

Vivekachudâmaṇi.

DLXXXVI—DLXXXVII.

THE knower and the ignorant are both equally subject each to his own previous *Karma* ;—the knower, all patience, knows no sorrow, the ignorant, ever unsteady, continues to grieve. Of two men passing on the road, both being equally fatigued and the road before them being equal,

---

* नित्यानुभवरूपस्य को मे वानुभवः पृथक् ।
कृतं कृत्यं प्रापणीयं प्राप्तमित्येव निश्चयः ॥

पञ्चदशी.

† कर्त्तापि वा कारयितापि नाहं
भोक्तापि वा भोजयितापि नाहम् ।
द्रष्टापि वा दर्शयितापि नाहं
सोऽहं स्वयंज्योतिरनीदृगात्मा ॥

विवेकचूडामणिः.

he that knows treads on patiently to the end, the poor ignorant fool lingers behind bemoaning his lot.*

Panchadasi.

DLXXXVIII—DLXXXIX.

BLISS here attends the extremes of Intellect;—the highest which transcends Intellect, and the lowest which is far below Intellect. The way between these extremes is the way of worry and evil. A very thin partition divides ecstacy from madness; for, in the former, the mind having lost all faith is quite clear of every tinge of attachment.†

Bhâgavata; Yogavâsistha.

DXC.

IN all acts whatever, whether of commission or omission there is nothing, save absence of attachment, to distinguish the fool from the man of wisdom.‡

Yogavâsistha.

---

* ज्ञानिनोऽज्ञानिनश्चात्र समे प्रारब्धकर्मणी ।
न क्लेशो ज्ञानिनो धैर्यान्मूढः क्लिश्यत्यधैर्यतः ॥
मार्गे गन्त्रोर्द्वयोः श्रान्तौ समायामप्यदूरताम् ।
जानन्धैर्याद्द्रुतं गच्छेदन्यास्तिष्ठति दीनधीः ॥

पञ्चदशी.

† यश्च मूढतमो लोके यश्च बुद्धेः परं गतः ।
तावुभौ सुखमेधेते क्लिश्यत्यन्तरितो जनः ॥

भागवतम्.

एक एव विशेषोऽस्य न समो मूढबुद्धिभिः ।
सर्वत्रास्थापरित्यागान्नीरागममलं मनः ॥

योगवासिष्ठम्.

‡ तज्ज्ञाज्ञयोरशेषेषु भावाभावेषु कर्मसु ।
ऋते निर्वासनत्वात्तु न विशेषोऽस्ति कश्चन ॥

योगवासिष्ठम्.

DXCI.

I look with equal eye upon a poisonous snake or a garland of flowers, upon a strong enemy or a kind friend, upon a costly jewel or a lump of earth, a bed of flowers or a slab of stone, a group of beautiful women or a collection of useless straw;—thus do I spend all my days in some holy solitude, all intent on the blissful syllable S'iva, S'iva, S'iva.*

Bhartṛhari.

DXCII.

NEITHER action nor inaction are in me, ever one and without parts; how can he act who is all one Self, a compact mass, all-full and all-filling like the *Âkâśa*.†

Vivekachudamaṇi.

DXCIII.

HE is never overjoyed though often coming to good things; he stands firm as Meru under the direst calamity; he

---

* अहौ वा हारे वा बलवति रिपौ वा सुहृदि वा
मणौ वा लोष्ठे वा कुसुमशयने वा दृषदि वा ।
तृणे वा स्त्रैणे वा मम समदृशो यान्ति दिवसाः
क्वचित्पुण्येऽरण्ये शिव शिव शिवेति प्रलपतः ॥

भर्तृहरिः.

† न मे प्रवृत्तिर्न च मे निवृत्तिः
सदैकरूपस्य निरंशकस्य ।
एकात्मको यो निबिडो निरन्तरो
व्योमेव पूर्णः स कथं नु चेष्टते ॥

विवेकचूडामणिः.

walks the world like a god, finding Self in the bliss of Self in every thing whatever.*

Svâsâjyasiddhi.

DXCIV.

A *Chânḍâla*, a twice-born, a *S'udra*, an ascetic, a man of intellect refined by application to *gnosis*, the lord of *Yogins*;—thus described at the top of thoughtless prattle by men conceiving each his own fancy, sages harmonised in the Self wend their way neither angry nor proud of the compliments thus bestowed.†

Bhartṛhari.

DXCV.

THE knower catches in the ecstacy of his heart the full light of that *Brahman* which is indescribable, all thought, all pure bliss, incomparable, transcending time, ever free, beyond desire, resembling limitless *Âkâśa*, having no parts and admitting of no idea beside itself.‡

Vivekachudamaṇi.

---

* न प्रहृष्यत्यसौ प्राप्य भूयः प्रियं
मेरुवन्निश्चलो भूरिकृच्छ्रेष्वपि
भावयन्नात्मनात्मानमानन्दितो
देववत्संचरत्येव विश्वम्भराम् ॥

स्वाराज्यसिद्धिः.

† चाण्डालः किमयं द्विजातिरथवा शूद्रोऽथ किं तापसः
किं वा तत्त्वनिवेशपेशलमतिर्योगीश्वरः कोऽपि किम् ।
इत्युत्पन्नविकल्पजल्पमुखरैः सम्भाष्यमाणा जनै-
र्न क्रुद्धाः पथि नैव तुष्टमनसो यान्ति स्वयं योगिनः ॥

भर्तृहरिः.

‡ किमपि सततबोधं केवलानन्दरूपं
निरुपममतिवेलं नित्यमुक्तं निरीहम् ।
निरवधिगगनाभं निष्कलं निर्विकल्पं
हृदि कलयति विद्वान् ब्रह्म पूर्णं समाधौ ॥

विवेकचूडामणिः.

DXCVI—DXCVII.

DOES it make any difference in this gem of heaven, the sun, if he is reflected in the waters of the Ganges or in the stream flowing through the scavenger's street? Does it make any difference in the *Âkâśa* enclosed in an earthenware or in a jar of gold? In that Thing, the inner being of all, the billowless ocean of native bliss and light, what means this great delusion, this nightmare of separateness, creating distinctions of *Brâhmaṇa* and *Chânḍâla* and so on. The self-same consciousness shines plainly in all the three conditions of waking, dream and sleep; it is, moreover, the inner witness of all,—pervading even like a thread, all forms whatever from Brahmâ to the tinniest ant;—He who has the firm conviction 'I am this consciousness', not the form it takes, let him be a *Brâhmaṇa* or a *Chânḍâla*, my mind points to him as the real Master.*

S'ankarâchârya.

DXCVIII.

HAS it set! is it broken! is it shattered to pieces! is it dissolved! is it pounded to dust! is it swallowed up! is it suddenly gone to decay!—the mind being put out, I

---

* किं गङ्गाम्बुनि बिम्बितेऽम्बरमणौ चाण्डालवाटीपयः-
पूरे वान्तरमस्ति काञ्चनघटीमृत्कुम्भयोर्वाम्बरे ।
प्रत्यग्वस्तुनि निस्तरङ्गसहजानन्दावबोधाम्बुधौ
विप्रोऽयं श्वपचोऽयमित्यपि महान् कोऽयं विभेदभ्रमः ॥
जाग्रत्स्वप्नसुषुप्तिषु स्फुटतरा या संविदुज्जृम्भते
या ब्रह्मादिपिपीलिकान्ततनुषु प्रोता जगत्साक्षिणी ।
सैवाहं न च दृश्यवस्त्विति दृढप्रज्ञापि यस्यास्ति चे-
च्चाण्डालोऽस्तु स तु द्विजोऽस्तु गुरुरित्येषा मनीषा मम ॥

मनीषापञ्चकम्.

do not find even a trace of the universe in the free depths of my-self, the indescribable ocean of the bliss of Self-realization.*

Svârâjyasiddhi.

DXCIX.

ALL latent desire having died out, he looks upon the world as all destroyed, as some unreal nightmare, as a castle-in-the-air, or even as a painting which is nearly washed off under a heavy downpour of rain.†

Yogavâsishtha.

DC.

BRAHMAN is the dedication and *Brahman* the offering; *Brahman* is the fire and *Brahman* the sacrificer; it must find its way to *Brahman* through this ecstacy of action which is *Brahman*.‡

Bhagvadgitâ.

---

* किमस्तं किं ध्वस्तं किमु विलुलितं किन्नु गलितं
विशीर्णं वा गीर्णं ननु सपदि जीर्णं किमथ वा ।
अमन्दे स्वच्छन्दे निरुपमनिजानन्दजलधौ
मयि स्वान्ते शान्ते जगदिदमशेषं न कलये ॥

स्वाराज्यसिद्धिः.

† उद्ध्वस्तमसदाभासमुत्पन्ननगरोपमम् ।
वर्षप्रोन्मृष्टचित्राभं जगत्पश्यत्यवासनः ॥

योगवासिष्ठम्.

‡ ब्रह्मार्पणंब्रह्महविर्ब्रह्माग्नौ ब्रह्मणा हुतम् ।
ब्रह्मैव तेन गन्तव्यं ब्रह्मकर्मसमाधिना ॥

भगवद्गीता.

1.—Jivanmukti.

DCI—DCV.

THOUGH ever moving about in the world of experience; the whole of it exists not for him ;—all-pervading ether-like consciousness alone subsists. Such a one is called *Jivanmukta.* The expression of his countenance neither fluses nor fades under pleasure or pain, he stands unmoved whatever may come or go. Such a one is called *Jivanmukta.* Though acting after every feeling, such as love, hate, fear and the like, he who stands unaffected within like the *Âkâśa*, is said to be the real *Jivanmukta* (liberated while yet in this life). He whom the world finds no cause to fear, and who is never afraid of the world, ever beyond joy, and jealousy, and fear, is said to be the real *Jivanmukta.* With the woes of this world laid entirely at rest, he who, though full of all learning and art is yet without any, who, though with mind is without it, is said to be the real *Jivanmukta.**

Yogavâsishtha.

---

* यथास्थितमिदं यस्य व्यवहारवतोऽपि च ।
अस्तं गतं स्थितं व्योम स जीवन्मुक्त उच्यते ॥
नोदेति नास्तमायाति सुखदुःखैर्मुखप्रभा ।
यथाप्राप्ते स्थितिर्यस्य स जीवन्मुक्त उच्यते ॥
रागद्वेषभयादीनामनुरूपं चरन्नपि ।
योऽन्तर्व्योमवदत्यच्छः स जीवन्मुक्त उच्यते ॥
यस्मान्नोद्विजते लोको लोकान्नोद्विजते च यः ।
हर्षामर्षभयोन्मुक्तः स जीवन्मुक्त उच्यते ॥
शान्तसंसारकलनः कलावानपि निष्कलः ।
यः सचित्तोऽपि निश्चित्तः स जीवन्मुक्त उच्यते ॥

योगवासिष्ठम् ।

DCVI—DCVIII.

TREMBLING and other signs of fear subside, only by degrees, even after knowledge of the snake as nothing but a harmless piece of rope; the same rope met with in dim light, even after such knowledge, may yet become the same terrible snake it once was. Thus previous *Karma* comes gradually to end by fruition through experience and not all at once by any obstinate remedy; nay, it is even possible for the immortal one to temporarily feel his mortality in moments of such fruition. This, however, is no flaw in the condition of *gnosis* once realized, for, *Jivanmukti* is no observance, it is being at harmony with the course of nature.*

Panchadas'i.

DCIX—DCX.

ALL even in weal or woe; all peace; looking with equal eye on a lump of earth or a mass of gold; unaffected by likes or dislikes; unmoved by praise or censure; all patience; untouched by respect or contempt; even-minded towards friends or foes; initiating no act whatever;—such a one has really risen beyond the *Guṇas.*†

Bhagavadgitâ.

---

* रज्जुज्ञानेऽपि कम्पादिः शनैरेवोपशाम्यति ।
पुनर्मन्दान्धकारे सा रज्जुः क्षिप्तोरगी भवेत् ॥
एवमारब्धभोगोऽपि शनैः शाम्यति नो हठात् ।
भोगकाले कदाचित्तु मर्त्योऽहमिति भासते ॥
नैतावताऽपराधेन तत्त्वज्ञानं विनश्यति ।
जीवन्मुक्तिव्रतं नेदं किन्तु वस्तुस्थितिः खलु ॥

पञ्चदशी.

† समदुःखसुखः स्वस्थः समलोष्टाश्मकाञ्चनः ।
तुल्यप्रियाप्रियो धीरस्तुल्यनिन्दात्मसंस्तुतिः ॥
मानापमानयोस्तुल्यस्तुल्यो मित्रारिपक्षयोः ।
सर्वारम्भपरित्यागी गुणातीतः स उच्यते ॥

भगवद्गीता.

DCXI—DCXII.

WHEN all desires infesting the heart are entirely given up, the mortal becomes immortal and lives in *Brahman* even here. The slough cast off by the serpent lies dead and lifeless on the ant-hill; so even lies this body; and the mortal who is thus disembodied, while yet here, becomes immortal, all life, all *Brahman*, all light.*

Bṛhadâraṇyakopanishad.

DCXIII.

THE man of spiritual wisdom has acquired the eye which looks evenly on a *Brâhmaṇa* full of learning and virtue, on a cow, on an elephant, on a dog, or on a low out-cast.†

Bhagavadgitâ.

DCXIV.

THE highest Self, all endless bliss, unconditioned limitless consciousness, being realized, whether through the great texts‡ or through *Yoga*, in all experience whatever, let (him)

---

* यदा सर्वे प्रमुच्यन्ते कामा येऽस्य हृदि श्रिताः ।
अथ मर्त्योऽमृतो भवत्यत्र ब्रह्म समश्नुत इति ॥
तद्यथाहिनिर्ल्वयनी वल्मीके मृताप्रत्यस्ता शयीतैवमेवेदं शरीरं शेते अथायमशरीरोऽमृतः प्राणो ब्रह्मैव तेज एव ।

बृहदारण्यकोपनिषत्.

† विद्याविनयसम्पन्ने ब्राह्मणे गवि हस्तिनि ।
शुनि चैव श्वपाके च पण्डिताः समदर्शिनः ॥

भगवद्गीता.

‡ The great texts are such as 'Thou art That' and the like, teaching unity of consciousness throughout the world of subject and object.

lose himself in the ecstacy of trance or in deep intercourse with the world, nay let him freely enjoy every object of sense;—he has for ever lost all touch with bondage (of every description).*

Svârâjyasiddhi.

DCXV.

EVEN the body is subject to the law of *Karma*, it awaits the fulfilment of the life it embodies only as long as the causes of its existence endure. This body along with the world of experience connected with it, he never minds who has acquired the condition of ecstatic trance; he never thinks of dream-experience who is awakened to the light of Truth.†

The Bhâgavata.

DCXVI.

ALL content with what gain chance brings to him, ever beyond all duality, completely free from envy and hate, equal in success or defeat,—he *acts* without relating himself to the act.‡

Bhagavadgitâ.

---

* निरवधिसुखभूमानन्तसंवित्परात्म-
न्यनुभवमधिरूढे वाक्यतो योगतो वा ।
भवतु दृढसमाधिर्लोकसंग्राहको वा
भजतु विषयजातं नैति भूयोऽपि बन्धम् ॥

स्वाराज्यसिद्धिः.

† देहोऽपि दैववशगः खलु कर्म यावत्
स्वारम्भकं प्रतिसमीक्षत एव सासुः ।
तं सप्रपञ्चमधिरूढसमाधियोगः
स्वाप्नं पुनर्न भजते प्रतिबुद्धवस्तुः ॥

भागवतम्.

‡ यदृच्छालाभसन्तुष्टो द्वन्द्वातीतो विमत्सरः ।
समः सिद्धावसिद्धौ च कृत्वापि न निबध्यते ॥

भगवद्गीता.

DCXVII.

CLAD in rich cloth or in the wide expanse of space, having his skin alone for cover or buried deep in the ample folds of all-embracing thought,—he wanders the world like a mad man,—like a child, or even like a ghost.*

Vivekachudâmaṇi.

DCXVIII.

WITHOUT having in one's Self the clear light of Self-experience, no one can appreciate the phenomenal sublimity of another's experience in the same line;—The *Brâhmaṇa* cannot understand the sweets of wine†.‡

Yogavâsishtha.

DCXIX—DCXX.

THE knower harmonised in the Essence should never think he did anything. Whether he sees, hears, touches, smells, walks, sleeps, breathes, speaks, gives, takes, or even performs

---

दिगम्बरो वापि च साम्बरो वा
त्वगम्बरो वापि चिदम्बरस्थः ।
उन्मत्तवद् वापि च बालवद् वा
पिशाचवद् वापि चरत्यवन्याम् ॥

विवेकचूडामणिः

† For he is prohibited from using wine which Kshatriyas and others may use.

‡ परमार्थचमत्कारमन्तस्यानुभवं विना ।
अन्यस्यान्यं न जानाति सीधु स्वादुमिव द्विजः ॥

योगवासिष्ठम्.

such involuntary acts as the closing and opening of the eyelids,—he should always think of the act as not his, but of the senses which pass out, of themselves, to their respective objects.*

Bhagavadgitâ.

DCXXI.

AS timber is carried away by the stream to places high and low, so even is the body led by Fate to whatever awaits it at its proper time.†

Vivekachudâmaṇi.

DCXXII.

THE traveller with mind firmly fixed only on the goal he is approaching, never feels the motion of his legs along the road he treads ; act thus in all you do.‡

Yogavâsishtha.

---

* नैव किंचित्करोमीति युक्तो मन्येत तत्त्ववित् ।
पश्यञ्शृण्वन्स्पृशञ्जिघ्रन्नश्नन्गच्छन्स्वपञ्श्वसन् ॥
प्रलपन्विसृजन्गृह्णन्नुन्मिषन्निमिषन्नपि ।
इन्द्रियाणीन्द्रियार्थेषु वर्तन्त इति धारयन् ॥

भगवद्गीता.

† स्रोतसा नीयते दारु यथा निम्नोन्नतस्थलम् ।
दैवेन नीयते देहो यथाकालोपभुक्तिषु ॥

विवेकचूडामणिः.

‡ गन्तव्यदेशैकनिष्ठस्य यथा पान्थस्य पादयोः ।
स्पन्दो विगतसङ्कल्पस्तथास्पन्दस्व कर्मसु ॥

योगवासिष्ठम्.

DCXXIII.

THE fright caused by the appearance of a thief survives his capture, the cloth yet leaves the impress of its form on the ashes to which it is burnt;—the world reduced of itself to naught in the case of the Knower lasts with his body to bear out such fruition as previous *Karma* should bring.*

Svârâjyasiddhi.

DCXXIV.

THE knower may, oh child! let his external senses loose in all acts and all conditions whatever as long as his body lasts; but he should never let his internal sense go with the external.†

Yogavâsishtha.

DCXXV.

THE *Âkâśa* may appear in any condition whatever, it is never conditioned; the silent one never takes on the

---

* चोरबाधेऽपि तज्जन्यभीत्यादिव-
चेलदाहेऽपि भस्मेव चेलाकृति ।
ज्ञानिनां विश्वमादेहपातं स्वतो
बाधितत्वेऽपि चारब्धभोगक्षमम् ॥

स्वाराज्यसिद्धिः.

† यावद्देहं यथाचारं दशास्वङ्ग विजानता ।
कर्मेन्द्रियैर्हि स्थातव्यं न तु बुद्धीन्द्रियैः क्वचित् ॥

योगवासिष्ठम्.

properties of whatever accidents may appear to colour his Self:—he may stand like a fool though all-knowing, he may act after the air ever untainted.*

Atmabodha.

DCXXVI.

BHARATA and others never stood like wood or stone giving up food and other necessaries; they were indifferent being afraid of the possibility of attachment.†

Panchadas'i.

DCXXVII.

THE act never touches me, nor do I ever desire any result from the act;—he who thus reads my secret is never bound by action.‡

Bhagavadgitâ.

---

* उपाधिस्थोऽपि तद्धर्मैर्न लिप्तो व्योमवन्मुनिः ।
सर्वविन्मूढवत्तिष्ठेदसक्तो वायुवच्चरेत् ॥

आत्मबोधः.

† न आहारादि संत्यज्य भरताद्याः स्थिताः क्वचित् ।
काष्ठपाषाणवत्किन्तु संगभीता उदासते ॥

पञ्चदशी.

‡ न मां कर्माणि लिम्पन्ति न मे कर्मफले स्पृहा ।
इति मां योऽभिजानाति कर्मभिर्न स बध्यते ॥

भगवद्गीता.

DCXXVIII—DCXXX.

THE knowers of the supreme neither avoid nor court intercourse with the world, they go with whatever should turn up in ordinary course. Being in all, I am ever inactive :—he who, with this conviction, acts in accord with what is brought to him in the course of nature is always inactive. He is not motionless though standing ; he does not walk though going; he is all peace though deep in intercourse; he is ever inactive though full of activity.*

Yogavâsishtha.

DCXXXI.

THE world follows the lead of great souls in what they do; whatever they sanction men accept.†

Bhagavadgitâ.

---

* न त्यजन्ति न वाञ्छन्ति व्यवहारं जगद्गतम् ।
सर्वमेवानुवर्तन्ते पारावारविदो जनाः ॥
सर्वस्थोऽहमकर्तेति दृढभावनयानया ।
प्रवाहपतितं कार्यं कुर्वन्नपि न लिप्यते ॥
तिष्ठन्नपि हि नासीनो गच्छन्नपि न गच्छति ।
शान्तोऽपि व्यवहारस्थः कुर्वन्नपि न लिप्यते ॥

योगवासिष्ठम्.

† यद्यदाचरति श्रेष्ठस्तत्तदेवेतरो जनः ।
स यत्प्रमाणं कुरुते लोकस्तदनुवर्तते ॥

भगवद्गीता.

DCXXXII.

THIS kind of apparent 'latent desire' in those who have found liberation while living is no desire at all; it is that universal sense of *being* which is known as 'pure *Satva*.'*

Yogavâsishtha.

DCXXXIII—DCXXXIV.

AS the uninformed act *with attachment*, so should, oh Bhârata! the informed act *without attachment*; for, thus alone could he do good to the world. Do not unsettle the intellect of the uninformed attached to the course of *action*; the informed going by the light of inner discrimination should show himself favourable to all acts whatever.†

Bhagavadgitá.

---

* येयं तु जीवन्मुक्तानां वासना सा न वासना ।
शुद्धसत्त्वाभिधानं तत् सत्तासामान्यमुच्यते ॥

योगवासिष्ठम्.

† सक्ताः कर्मण्यविद्वांसो यथा कुर्वन्ति भारत ।
कुर्याद्विद्वांस्तथासक्तश्चिकीर्षुर्लोकसङ्ग्रहम् ॥
न बुद्धिभेदं जनयेदज्ञानां कर्मसङ्गिनाम् ।
जोषयेत्सर्वकर्माणि विद्वान्युक्तः समाचरन् ॥

भगवद्गीता.

DCXXXV—DCXXXVI.

HAVING known It thus, fill thyself with the memory of pure Unity; having realized the Unit, walk the world like a mass of so much (dead) matter. No praise, no salute, no offerings (even) to the dead, no fixed or unfixed abode,—the harmonised (soul) should ever live by chance.*

Gaudapâdâchârya.

DCXXXVII.

TAKE no thought of the result, rest ever content, yearn not for any support;—plunge thyself thus deep in any action whatever, thou art ever free.†

Bhagavadgitâ.

---

ii.—Videhamukti.

DCXXXVIII—DCXL.

THE fifteen rays‡ return into their source, the divine forces governing the senses find back the universal fountain of

---

* तस्मादेवं विदित्वैनमद्वैते योजयेत् स्मृतिम् ।
अद्वैतं समनुप्राप्य जडवल्लोकमाचरेत् ॥
निस्तुतिर्निर्नमस्कारो निःस्वधाकार एव च ।
चलाचलनिकेतश्च यतिर्यादृच्छिको भवेत् ॥

गौडपादाचार्याः.

† त्यक्त्वा कर्मफलासङ्गं नित्यतृप्तो निराश्रयः ।
कर्मण्यभिप्रवृत्तोऽपि नैव किञ्चित्करोति सः ॥

भगवद्गीता.

‡ Will, idea, *A'kâs'a*, *Vâyu*, *Tejas*, *Jala*, *Pṛthvi*, (inner and outer) senses, mind; (on the objective plane) food, energy; *mantras*, austerities; worlds, inhabitants, names. These sixteen are mentioned in the *Prashnopanishad*.

their rise, the reflection in the inner sense—the embodied soul —together with every action whatever, all become one in the supreme unchangeable (Essence). As rivers flowing into the ocean lose their individual name and form, nay thus lose even themselves, so does the *knower*, freed from all name and all form, find the highest Being, all light. He who thus *knows* the highest *Brahman*, verily becomes *Brahman*: none that is born in his family has his eye closed to *Brahman*. He sores above sin and sorrow; freed from the ties of the heart, he becomes immortal.*

Muṇḍakopanishad.

DCXLI.

GIVING up the body in some holy place or in the house of a *Chânḍâla*, conscious or unconscious, he finds *Kaivalya*, all cause of sorrow being entirely destroyed, and liberation being found in the very moment of the rise of *gnosis*.†

Vârtika.

---

* गताः कलाः पञ्चदश प्रतिष्ठा
देवाश्च सर्वे प्रतिदेवतासु ।
कर्माणि विज्ञानमयश्च आत्मा
परेऽव्यये सर्व एकीभवन्ति ॥
यथा नद्यः स्यन्दमानाः समुद्रे-
ऽस्तं गच्छन्ति नामरूपे विहाय ।
तथा विद्वान्नामरूपाद्विमुक्तः
परात्परं पुरुषमुपैति दिव्यम् ॥
स यो ह वै तत्परमं ब्रह्म वेद ब्रह्मैव भवति नास्याब्रह्मवित्कुले भवति
तरति शोकं तरति पाप्मानं गुहाग्रन्थिभ्यो विमुक्तोऽमृतो भवति ॥
मुण्डकोपनिषद्.

† तीर्थे श्वपचगृहे वा नष्टस्मृतिरपि परित्यजन्देहम् ।
ज्ञानसमकालमुक्तः कैवल्यं याति हतशोकः ॥
वार्तिकम्.

DCXLII—DCXLIII.

WATER is water, whether it stands all placid or surges up in high billows; it makes no difference in the ocean. Embodied or disembodied, there is no difference in the liberation of the silent knower. What difference can embodiment or disembodiment make in the liberated, all Thought? Whether in tempestuous waves or in placid calm, the sameness of water undergoes no change.*

Yogavâsishtha.

DCXLIV.

OH Arjuna! the worlds even up to the sphere of *Brahman* are subject to the law of rise and set; having found Me, oh Son of Kunti! there is no rise and no set.†

Bhagavadgitâ.

DCXLV.

WHO has no desire, who is beyond desire, who has all desires fulfilled in the Supreme, who has Self as the object of all and every desire;—his breath rises not beyond him; being *Brahman*, he becomes *Brahman*.‡

Bṛhadâraṇyakopanishad.

---

* सौम्याम्बुत्वे तरङ्गत्वे सलिलस्याम्बुता यथा ।
समैवाब्धौ तथादेहसदेहमुनिमुक्तता ॥
सदेहादेहमुक्तानां भेदः को बोधरूपिणाम् ।
यदेवाम्बु तरङ्गत्वे सौम्यत्वेऽपि तदेव तत् ॥

योगवासिष्ठम्.

† आ ब्रह्मभुवनाल्लोकाः पुनरावर्तिनोऽर्जुन ।
मामुपेत्य तु कौन्तेय पुनर्जन्म न विद्यते ॥

भगवद्गीता.

‡ योऽकामो निष्काम आप्तकाम आत्मकामो ।
न तस्य प्राणा उत्क्रामन्ति ब्रह्मैव सन् ब्रह्माप्येति ॥

बृहदारण्यकोपनिषत्.

DCXLVI.

I have no *Mâyâ* for my consort, no serpent for my couch, no discuss for my weapon, no round of incarnations to go through, nor have I the anxiety of protecting the world, still I am the Lord Vishṇu to all intent and purpose.*

Svârâjyasiddhi.

DCXLVII—DCLI.

THE *Videhamuka* neither rises nor sets, nay he is never laid at rest. He is not *being* nor non-*being*, neither near nor distant, neither I nor thou. He shines as the sun, he protects the three worlds appearing as Vishṇu, as Rudra he destroys all, he acts the creator in the form of the lotus-born Prajâpati. Whatever is, whatever has been, whatever shall be,—every object in any one of the three forms of Time—he is that; he is everything. Oh best of knowers! when the *Videhamukta* takes on the form of the three worlds and all they contain, I believe him to have gone through the act of creation. If verily the three worlds do exist, let him by all

---

* अहं न मायी न च भोगिशायी
न चक्रधारी न दशावतारी।
न मे प्रपञ्चः परिपालनीय-
स्तथापि विष्णुः प्रभविष्णुरस्मि॥

स्वाराज्यसिद्धिः.

means become those words, for *in* him the words "Three worlds" are, in truth, empty of all real content whatever.*

Yogavâsishtha.

DCLII.

THEY divert themselves in the native bliss of self-experience, they enjoy themselves in any manner with perfect freedom;—the many-sided, wonderful course the United pursue, on the inscrutable Path, ever free of attachment, knowing no limit, always tending to the good of the universe, is as inscrutable as the course of fishes in water, the passage of birds in the atmosphere, or the course of wind throughout space.†

Svârâjyasiddhi.

---

* विदेहमुक्तो नोदेति नास्तमेति न शाम्यति ।
न सन्नासन्न दूरस्थो न चाहं नापि चेतरः ॥
सूर्यो भूत्वा प्रतपति विष्णुः पाति जगत्त्रयम् ।
रुद्रः सर्वान्संहरति सर्गान्सृजति पद्मजः ॥
यत्किञ्चिदिदमाभाति भातं भानमुपैष्यति ।
कालत्रयगतं दृश्यं तदसौ सर्वमेव च ॥
विदेहमुक्तास्त्रैलोक्यं संपद्यन्ते यदा तदा ।
मन्ये ते सर्गतामेव गता वेदविदां वर ॥
विद्यते येषु त्रिभुवनं तत्तत्तां सम्प्रयान्तु ते ।
यत्र त्रैलोक्यशब्दार्थौ न सम्भवति कश्चन ॥

योगवासिष्ठम्.

† स्वानन्दे सहजे सदा विहरतां स्वच्छन्दलीलाजुषां
निस्सङ्गा च निरर्गला च जगतां कल्याणसन्दोहिनी ।
मत्स्यानां सलिलेऽम्बरे च वयसां वायोरिवाशामुखे
दुर्लक्ष्ये पथि योगिनां बहुविधा गूढा विचित्रा गतिः ॥

स्वाराज्यसिद्धिः.

DCLIII—DCLIV.

WHENEVER, oh Bhârata! Truth is on the decline, and Untruth appears to succeed, I create myself to guide the good, destroy the wicked, and strengthen the foundation of Truth. Thus do I appear from cycle to cycle.*

Bhagavadgitâ.

VI.—CONCLUSION.

DCLV.

DOUBT, dispute and explanation, all depend on language which means duality. In the language of Unity, there can be no question and no answer.†

Panchadas'i.

---

* यदा यदा हि धर्मस्य ग्लानिर्भवति भारत ।
अभ्युत्थानमधर्मस्य तदाऽऽत्मानं सृजाम्यहम् ॥
परित्राणाय साधूनां विनाशाय च दुष्कृताम् ।
धर्मसंस्थापनार्थाय संभवामि युगे युगे ॥

भगवद्गीता.

† चोद्यं वा परिहारो वा क्रियतां द्वैतभाषया ।
अद्वैतभाषया चोद्यं नास्ति नापि तदुत्तरम् ॥

पञ्चदशी.

DCLVI.

THERE is no dissolution, no creation, none in bondage, no pupilage, none desirous of liberation, none liberated ;—this is the Absolute Truth.*

Gaudapâdâchârya.

DCLVII.

BOW to him who enunciated this method of harmony in the Absolute, conducing to the well-being of all, beneficent, above all dispute, entirely non-antithetical.†

Gaudapâdâchârya.

DCLVIII.

WONDERFUL, supremely wonderful—this Philosophy! More wonderful still the Masters who teach the Truth! A thousand wonders surround the depth of GNOSIS taught! The bliss of Knowledge is the Silence of indescribable wonder!‡

Panchadas'i.

---

* न निरोधो नचोत्पत्तिर्न बद्धो न च साधकः ।
न मुमुक्षुर्न वै मुक्त इत्येषा परमार्थता ॥

गौडपादाचार्याः.

† अस्पर्शयोगो वै नाम सर्वसत्त्वसुखो हितः ।
अविवादोऽविरुद्धश्च देशितस्तं नमाम्यहम् ॥

गौडपादाचार्याः.

‡ अहो शास्त्रमहो शास्त्रमहो गुरुरहो गुरुः ।
अहो ज्ञानमहो ज्ञानमहो सुखमहो सुखम् ॥

पञ्चदशी.

BOMBAY—PRINTED AT THE "TATVA-VIVECHAKA" PRESS.

I—INDEX.

LIST OF WORKS CONSULTED.

अपरोक्षानुभूतिः	अप०	निर्वाणदशकम्	नि० द०
आत्मचिन्तनम्	आ० चिं०	नैष्कर्म्यसिद्धिः	नै० सि०
आत्मपुराणम्	आ० पु०	पञ्चतन्त्रम्	पंच०
आत्मबोधः	आ० बो०	पञ्चदशी	प०
आत्मषट्कम्	आ० ष०	परापूजा	प० पू०
आनन्दलहरिः	आ० ल०	प्रश्नोपनिषत्	प्र० उ०
ईशोपनिषत्	ई० उ०	प्रास्ताविकः	प्रा०
उत्तरगीता	उ० गी०	बृहदारण्यकोपनिषत्	बृ० उ०
उपदेशसाहस्त्री	उ० सा०	भगवद्गीता	भ० गी०
ऐतरेयोपनिषत्	ऐ० उ०	भागवतम्	भा०
कठोपनिषत्	क० उ०	भामिनीविलासः	भा० वि०
काशीपञ्चकम्	का० प०	मनीषापञ्चकम्	म० प०
केनोपनिषत्	के० उ०	मनुस्मृतिः	म०
गौडपादकारिका	गौ०	महाभारतम्	म० भा०
चर्पटपञ्जरिका	च० प०	महिम्नःस्तोत्रम्	महि०
छान्दोग्योपनिषत्	छा० उ०	माण्डुक्योपनिषत्	मा० उ०
जीवन्मुक्तिविवेकः	जी० वि०	मुण्डकोपनिषत्	मु० उ०
ज्ञानाङ्कुशम्	ज्ञा०	मेधातिथिः	मे०
तैत्तिरीयोपनिषत्	तै० उ०	योगवासिष्ठम्	यो० वा०
दृग्दृश्यविवेकः	दृ० वि०	योगसूत्रम्	यो० सू०

26

वार्तिकम् .... वा०
विज्ञाननौका .... वि० नौ०
विवेकचूडामणिः .... वि० चू०
वैराग्यशतकम् .... वै० श०
व्यासस्मृतिः .... व्या०
शंकरः .... शं०
श्वेताश्वतरोपनिषत् .... श्वे० उ०
सप्तशती स० श०
स्मृतिः .... स्मृ०
स्वात्मनिरूपणम् .... स्वा० नि०
स्वाराज्यसिद्धिः .... स्वा० सि०
हठप्रदीपिका .... ह० प्र०
हरिमीडेस्तोत्रम् .... हरि०
हस्तामलकम् ह०

II—INDEX.

QUOTATIONS ALPHABETICALLY ARRANGED.

*** The numbers refer throughout to the number of the quotation.

ततोनजायतेकिञ्चि० आ० पु० 9-12

III—INDEX.

PRINCIPAL POINTS OF THE ABSOLUTE PHILOSOPHY.

IV—INDEX.

WORDS NOT ENGLISHED IN THE TEXT.

Anâtman—

Not-self; everything beside the unit of consciousness.

Apâna—

One of the five vital breaths; its seat is in the lower regions of the body.

Araṇi—

A plant of that name; two pieces of the wood of this plant rubbed one against the other produce fire.

Asurya—

A hell where the sun never shines; spiritually the condition of supreme ignorance.

Aśvattha—

The name of a sacred tree; that which does not stay till the morrow, whence this world, *Mâyâ*.

Atharva-veda—

One of the four Vedas.

Avidyâ—

That which is opposed to *Vidyâ*, light, gnosis; illusion; technically, individual ignorance.

Avyakta—

The material principle in nature, the second prolific member of the duality from which the Sânkhya-philosophy explains nature; the unmanifest; the undifferenced.

Âkâśa—

The first material *idea* from *Brahman*; the most subtle of the five elements.

Âśrama—

Place; position; one of the four periods over which human activity is distributed by the Hindu Scriptures.

Brahmâ—

The first Logos; creator; so-called in the *Purâṇas*.

Brahma-loka—

The world of *Brahman*.

Brahman—

The absolute Unit; universal Being; the All.

Brahma-vidyâ—

Science of *Brahman*; Gnosis.

Brâhmaṇa—

One who has realized *Brahman*; popularly one belonging to the highest of the four *Varṇas*.

Buddhi—

The discriminating sense in the inner mind; the first reflection of *Brahman*, in evolution.

Chândâla—

The child begotten by a *S'udra* upon a *Brâhmana* woman; one of low class.

Chidâkâśa—

See DLIII--DLV.

Ekarshi—

One of the several fires worshipped daily by the householder.

Ghee—

Clarified butter.

Gandharva—

A class of beings between gods and men.

Guṇa—

Property; particularly one of the three properties—light, energy, darkness—of Nature (*Prakṛti.*)

Hirṇyagarbha—

The cosmic manifestation of *Brahman* on the subtile plane.

Jaina—

The philosophy or follower of Jina; a philosophy emphasizing the idea of relativity, preaching universal compassion, and opposed to the *Brâhmaṇic* ritual and the *Veda*.

Jala—

Water; the fourth element from Âkâśa.

Jiva—

Individualized consciousness; every being whatever; individual manifestation of *Brahman* on the material plane; soul.

Jivan-mukti—

Liberation while yet living; realization of *Brahman* before death.

Kaivalya—

Isolation; technically that ideal condition of one-ness which embraces all distinction in itself; liberation according to the *Advaita* is so-called.

Karma—(*Karman*)

Act; technically the theory of cause and effect, the law of compensation; also the formal part of religion, called *Karma-mârga*.

Kes'ava—

The god Kṛshṇa.

Kshatriya—

One belonging to the second of the four *Varṇas*; one of the warrior class.

Kus'a—

A wild grass held supremely sacred, used in all religious ceremonies.

Mahâ-mâyâ—

The great power of illusion; often personified as a powerful Goddess in the *Purâṇas*.

Mahat—

The first evolute from the *Prakṛti* of the S'ankhya-philosophy; cosmic mind.

Mâyâ—

Illusion; technically the power of illusion accompanying the cosmic manifestation of *Brahman* on the causal plane.

Meru—

A fabulous mountain of that name supposed to be in the middle of the earth, and the abode of all gods; the diametre of the globe of this earth.

Mimânsâ—

One of the six schools of philosophy; the exegetic philosophy of the Veda.

Mlehchha—

One belonging to a class or country beyond the pale of *Aryâvarta*.

Nâchiketa—

The esoteric fire so-called after Nachicketas to whom the solar God of death revealed it.

Pâncharâtra—

An old sect of devotional worship supposed to be founded by *Nârada*.

Pâśupata—

The school of that name; *Pati*—lord—S'iva, is worshipped as the saviour of all *Paśus*—animals in bondage, *viz.* souls.

Paulkasa—

The child begotten by a *S'udra* upon a *Kshatriya* woman; one of low class.

Pippal—

The sacred tree of that name.

Pitṛ—

The lunar prototypes of humanity: invoked in all ceremonies after death of any member of a family, also on occasions of every auspicious ceremony.

Purâṇas—

Popular books giving the truths of religion in a form acceptable to the general masses.

Purusha—

The conscious principle in Nature according to the S'ankhya-philosophy; It is different with every being; It may correspond to soul.

Prajâpati—

See *Brahmâ*.

Prakṛti—

The material first cause of evolution according to the *Sânkhya*.

Pralaya—

Cosmic dissolution.

Prâṇâyâma—

Control of breath; the process of inhaling, retaining and exhaling the air.

Prasthâna—

Stay; technically one of the three (*Brahma-Sutras, Upanishads*, and *Bhagvad-Gitâ*) from which any new teacher must evolve his philosophy to make it acceptable.

Prithvi—

The fifth element from *Âkâśa*; the earth.

Râja-(Yoga)—

Union with the Luminious; spiritual *Yoga*; the royal road to *Yoga*.

Ṛg-veda—

The Veda consisting of *ṚKS*; The most ancient of the four Vedas.

ṚK.—

A metre of the name; any line from the *Ṛgveda*.

Rudra—

The god of that name.

S'aiva—

Follower or philosophy of those who believe in and worship god S'iva; its forms are mainly Tántric.

Sannyâsin—

One who is in the fourth *Aśrama*; one who has renounced the word after the formal manner.

Sattva—

The first of the three properties of *Sânkyan Prakṛti*.

Sádhana—

Means; technically the four means which prepare one to be able to apply himself to the *Vedânta*.

Sâma-veda—

One of the four *Vedas*.

Sânkhya—

The philosophy of that name; It starts with the assumption of a material (*Prakṛti*) and a conscious (*Purusha*) principl e in Nature.

S'âstra—

Religious book; scripture; technically a system, a philosophy.

S'irovrata—

An observance well-known in the followers of the *Atharva-Veda*; a peculiar worship of fire.

S'iva—

The God of that name; bliss; blissful.

Śmârta—

Depending on or derived from the *Smṛtis*; forming part of duties enjoined by the *Smṛtis*.

Smṛti—

The scripture of authority next to the *Veda* which is *S'ruti*; duties enjoined after the manner of past teaching.

S'ramaṇa—

A Buddhist religious mendicant.

S'rauta—

Depending on or derived from *S'ruti*; forming part of the religion enjoined by *S'ruti*.

S'ruti—

That which is delivered by oral tradition; the *Veda*; a text from the *Veda*.

S'yâmâka—

A kind of corn, the grains being very minutely small and slippery.

Tejas—

Light; the third element from *Âkâs'a*.

Upâsanâ—

Sitting in the act of invocation; devotional worship.

Vadavânala—

The fire supposed to be at the bottom of the ocean, and powerful to consume the whole universe.

Vaishṇava—

One belonging to the sect of that name; a follower of god *Vishṇu*.

Varṇa—

Colour; one of the four divisions of ancient Indian society.

Vâyu—

Air; the second element from *Âkâs'a*.

Veda—

The storehouse of knowledge; the holy scripture of India.

Vedânta—

End of the *Veda*; the *Upanishads*; the philosophy of the *Advaita*.

Videhamukti—

Literally liberation after death; Vidyâraṇya interprets it to mean liberation from future embodiment, gained at the very moment of Gnosis. See Jivanmuktiviveka; also this book DCXLI.

Vidyâ—

Knowledge, Gnosis; opposed to *Avidyâ*; the true Science, *viz.*, the philosophy of the *Advaita*.

Vishṇu—

The god of that name.

Yajur-veda—

One of the four *Vedas*.

Yati—

One who has control over his mind and senses; an ascetic.

Yoga—

Union; technically preventing transformation of the thinking principle.

Yogin—

One in *Yoga*, *i. e.*, one who has mastered or acquired *Yoga*.

"Undoubtedly a valuable contribution to our knowledge of the subject":—Prof. W. D. Whitney.

"The result of his labours is all that could have been desired. His full and yet very concise notes shew that he has thoroughly mastered the subject, and that he is also able to explain it to others."—Indian Antiquary (Dr. F. Kielhorn).

"Appears to be a very scholarly edition which is likely to supply a great want."—Dr. R. Rost (India Office).

"Find it very good."—Dr. G. Bühler.

"Himself deeply imbued with the system, and well-read in cognate literature, as also not unfamiliar with Western Logic, his interpretations are quite welcome. I recommend the young Sanskritist to go through it minutely and repeatedly."—Vienna Oriental Journal (Dr. H. Jacobi).

MONISM OR ADVAITISM?

(Price Rs. 2.)

Introduction to the Advaita-Philosophy in the light of Modern Speculation.

"Clever and thoughtful."—Sir R. West.

"I have examined your work with much interest."—E. B. Tylor.

"A very interesting contribution to the History of Indian Philosophy."—The Mind, London.

"The learned Prof. Dvivedi seems to admit that the principles of Advaita Philosophy find a very convenient expression in European Monism."—Open Court (Dr. P. Carus).

"The little work will be an interesting one for students of the Advaita."—Theosophist.

"The book is worth placing on every serious student's shelves."—Lucifer.

THE YOGA-SUTRAS.

(Price Rs. 1-8-0.)

(Copy-right of the first 1,000 given to the Theosophic Publication Fund, Bombay).

The aphorisms of Patanjali translated into English with copious Notes from different Commentaries.

"The best edition yet presented to the English-reading public."—Lucifer.

MÁNDUKYOPANISHAD.

(*Price Rs.* 1-8-0 .)

(Copy-right of the first 1,000 made over to the Theosophical Publication Fund, Bombay).

The *Mândukya* translated into English with Gaudapâda's *Karikâs* and Sankara's Gloss on both ; prefaced with an interesting critical Introduction.

"I am much delighted with the ability and keenness with which you treat your various subjects."—Dr. P. Carus.

"Mr. Dvivedi is a zealous champion of the Advaita system, and knows how to connect its formal teachings with all the grave questions of Modern Society."—The Monist.

" Mr. Dvivedi is to be congratulated on the ability and industry he has displayed.'—Theosophist.

SAMÁDHI-S'ATAKA.

(Copy-right of the first 500 given to the publisher, Mr. G. H., Ahmedabad.)

Sanskrit text of a Jaina book on the Nature and Study of the Soul, with English translation.

(IN PREPARATION.)

SYÁDVÁDA-MANJARI.

(Copy-right made over to the Government Educational Dept., Bombay.)

A Manual of Jaina Philosophy. Sanskrit text, with copious Notes, and Introduction.

(IN PREPARATION.)

STRAY THOUGHTS.

(*Comprising.*)

Hinduism A paper contributed to and read at the Parliament of Religions; published in the first volume of "The World's Parliament of Religions."

"A profound Philosopher."—Chicago Herald.

The Puranas (Published in Transactions of the International Congress of Orientalists, held at Stockholm, 1889). The Purâṇas explained in the light of Symbology as against Philology.

"The paper is learned and forcible, but is even more extraordinary for the perfection of its English. Such rich, mellow, varied, delicately-tinted diction might well be the envy of a cultivated native."—the Path.

Jainism and Brahmanism (A paper read at the International Congress of Orientalists, London, 1891, and awarded a Certificate of Merit)

The **Advaita Philosophy of S'ankara** (contributed to the Oriental Journal, Vienna)

Essays and Translations: Idol-Worship, S'anskâras, Garuda-Purâṇa, etc., and translations of Yâjnavalkya Yoga-Samhitâ, S'ruti-Sârasamuddharaṇa, etc., (contributed to 'the Oriental Department' — New York)

Suggestions (proposing changes in the text-books of the Government Educational Department)

Letters on Widow Re-marriage (Contributed to the Indian Papers)

Necessity of Spiritual Culture (a paper read before the 'Young Men's Association,' Baroda)

Contributions to the Theosophist, etc., and other Miscellaneous writings.

(IN THE PRESS.)

JIVAN-MUKTI-VIVEKA,

OR

THE PATH OF LIBERATION IN THIS LIFE.

(Copy-right of the first 1,000 given to the Theosophical Publication Fund, Bombay.)

Translation of a Sanskrit work of that name into English. It contains very useful instruction to students of spiritual *Yoga*.

GUJARATI BOOKS.

S'IKSHÂ-S'ATAKA (poems.)

MÂLATI-MÂDHAVA (translation.)

UTTARA-RÂMA-CHARITA (do.)

KÂNTÂ (A play.)

PURVA-DARS'ANA (a brief outline of Indian history.)

NÂRI-PRATISTHÂ (on the position of woman.)

PREMA-JIVANA (poems.)

SIDDHÂNTA-SÂRA (philosophy.)

PRÂṆAVINIMAYA (mesmerism.)

SANKSHIPTA-SUVÂKYA (translation.)

KÂVYA-MAYUKHA (poetics). In preparation.

THE SUDARS'ANA (Periodical Vol. XI.)

BÂLA-VILÂSA (moral essays.)

PARAMÂRGA-DARS'ANA (religious essays.)

CHÂRITRA (character.)

ABHEDORMI (poems.)

GULÂB-SINHA (novel). In press.

ÂTMANIMAJJANA (poems.)

BRÂHMAṆAS OF GUJARAT (essay.)

THE BHAGAVAD-GITÂ (translation and commentary.)

CRITICISM (essay.)

PANCHAS'ATI (philosophy.)

NYÂYA (Inductive logic). In preparation

Works undertaken and prepared on behalf of H. H. the Maharajah Gaekwar of Baroda:—

(*Translations from Sanskrit.*)

DVYÂS'RAYA (history.)

BHOJA-PRABANDHA (poetries.)

CHATURVINSHATI-PRABANDHA (history.)

VIKRAMA-CHARITA (tales.)

SAMÂDHI-S'ATAKA (philosophy.)

ANUBHAVA-PRADIPIKÂ (philosophy.)

S'RUTI-SÂRA-SAMUDDHARANA (philosophy.)

BUDDHI-SÂGARA (morals.)

TARKA-PARIBHÂSHÂ (logic.)

GORAKSHA-S'ATAKA (*Yoga.*)

SHAD-DARS'ANA-SAMUCHCHAYA (philosophy.)

SÂRA-SANGRAHA; No. I (abstract of historical works.)

SÂRA-SANGRAHA; No. II (do.)

PATTAN BHANDÂRAS (catalogue of books.)

VASTUPÂLA-CHARITA (biography.)

KUMÂRAPÂLA-CHARITA (biography.)

SAMARÂDITYCA-HARITA (releгious history). Incomplete.

YOGA-BINDU (*Yoga.*)

ANEKÂNTA-VÂDA-PRAVES'A (philosophy.)

(*Old Gujrati works edited.*)

PANCHOPÂKHYÂNA (translation.)

(*Sanskrit texts edited.*)

TARKA-PARIBHÂSHÂ (logic.)

ALAMKÂRA-CHUDÂMANI (rhetoric). Incomplete.

JYOTISHKARANDA (astronomy). Incomplete.

VṚTTARATNÂKARA WITH NEW COMMENTARY (prosody.)

S'ISUPÂLA-VADHA WITH NEW COM. (poem). Incomplete.

S'ṚNGÂRATILAKA OF RUDRA (poetry). Incomplete.

RASAMANJARI (rhetoric.)

CHHANDONUS'ASANA (prosody). Incomplete.

NAISHADHA WITH NEW COM. (poem). Incomplete.

SHADDARS'ANA-SAMUCHCHAYA (philosophy.)

SYADVÂDA-RATNÂKARÂVATARIKÂ (philosophy). Incomplete.

ANEKÂNTAVÂDA-PRAVES'A (philosophy.)

ABHINANDANA-KÂVYA (poem). Incomplete.

Compilations from English (Jnânamanjushâ-series.)

CHETANA-S'ASTRA (psychology.)

HISTORY OF SKRT. LITERATURE. In preparation.

(*Law Committee*).

VIVÂDA-TÂNDAVA (law) In preparation.

Translations undertaken and executed on behalf of H. H. the Rao of Kutch.

RHETORIC.

CULTURE AND SELF-CULTURE.

Work undertaken on behalf of the Gujrat Vernacular Society, Ahmedabad.

NYÂYA (deductive logic.) In preparation.